The Teaching of Reading

The Development of Literacy in the Early Years of School

Jeni Riley

P·C·P

Paul Chapman
Publishing Ltd

Copyright © 1996, Jeni Riley

All rights reserved

Paul Chapman Publishing Ltd
144 Liverpool Road
London
N1 1LA

British Library Cataloguing in Publication Data

Riley, Jeni
  The teaching of reading : the development of literacy in
  the early years of school
  1. Reading (Primary)
  I. Title
  372.4'14

  ISBN 1 85396 307 0

Typeset by Dorwyn Ltd, Rowlands Castle, Hants
Printed and bound in Great Britain

A B C D E F G H   9 8 7 6

Contents

*For Roy,
Nicky, Sacha and Benjamin*

Foreword

At a time when debates about the teaching of reading are again to the fore, Jeni Riley's informative discussion sheds a good deal of light on the issues which such debates throw up, particularly issues of teachers' knowledge, beliefs and practices.

The book clearly indicates the vast amount of knowledge which has been accumulated about reading and learning to read. Research has made major contributions to our knowledge of, for instance, the relationship between the learning or oral and written language and how these relationships can be exploited in helping children to bring together the different visual, auditory and contextual cues in learning to read.

Jeni Riley's book does far more than review and discuss the accumulated knowledge on early literacy development, however. A central feature of the book is the way she draws upon her own substantial research project into children's literacy development in the first year at school. Her research illustrates how knowledge can confront commonly held beliefs. The order of significance of four entry skills in 191 children in their first year at school was found to be the exact *reverse* of what their teachers believed it to be.

The book builds quickly on these findings to provide imaginative outlines of practices and resources which will promote early literacy development. The conviction of these suggestions reflects the author's background as a teacher and advisory teacher, as well as a teacher educator and researcher.

The Teaching of Reading is a distinctive book, unravelling knowledge, beliefs and practices and bringing them together again in a way which provides a source of pragmatic support and professional understanding: a combination which is needed perhaps more today than ever before.

Roger Beard
Reader in Literacy Education
University of Leeds

Acknowledgements

There are many people without whom this book would not have been written. First and foremost, I would like to thank the teachers and children who participated in my research project, without whom there would be less evidence to support the ideas this book attempts to promote.

Secondly, I am indebted to Professor Denis Lawton for his conviction that there was within my PhD thesis an interesting and important story to be told to a wider audience of teachers.

Thirdly, I would like to thank Dr Roger Beard, Reader in Literacy Education, University of Leeds, for writing the 'Foreword', for his scholarly advice and for reading and commenting on an early draft of the manuscript.

Many busy people have added their valuable perspectives: teachers, researchers and other specialists in the field of teaching literacy have helped to refine my ideas and offered comment on the drafts, all of which has added to the scope and integrity of the finished book. My thanks to Ruth Miskin of Kobi Nazrul School in Tower Hamlets, Shirley Bickler (Reading Recovery Co-ordinator in the Borough of Westminster) and Andrew Burrell.

I am grateful also to Louisa Power for her skilled polishing of my word-processed manuscript. The debt of thanks to my husband Roy is immense for his painstaking proof-reading and enduring enthusiasm for the endeavour.

Jeni Riley
April 1996

Introduction

Reading is important for society as well as the individual. Economics research has established that schooling is an investment that forms human capital — that is, knowledge, skill, and problem-solving ability that have enduring value. While a country receives a good return on investment in education at all levels from nursery school and kindergarten through college, the research reveals that the returns are highest from the early years of schooling when children are first learning to read . . . the early years set the stages for later learning. Without the ability to read, excellence in high school and beyond is unattainable.

(Commission on Reading, National Academy of Education, 1985, p. 1, cited in Adams, 1990)

The range and volume of publications contained in the literacy section of most educational libraries could be regarded as evidence that the story about the teaching of reading has been told. The production of yet another publication to add to these shelves might be seen as unnecessary and indeed foolish. It is the belief that serious gaps exist in the available literature that prompts this book. The necessity for the young child to become literate in the early years of school is indisputable.

First, the teaching of literacy remains riven with controversy despite the declaration made over ten years ago by Merritt (1985) that it is a debate that is 'long-past its bed-time'. Secondly, much political pressure, parental awareness and educational concern are expressed about the standard of literacy in primary schools and about the way in which it is taught: 'The wide gulf in pupils' reading performance is serious and unacceptable' (Ofsted, 1996, p. 7).

Thirdly, for too long the teaching of reading has been subjected to the world of opinion and fashion. There is no value in this. Robust research evidence exists regarding the efficacy of the methods that can usefully be employed in primary schools to support the teaching of reading. As Stainthorp (1992, p. 20) says, 'What concerns me far more is that good theory developed by cognitive psychologists is not actually filtering down to the people who need to know and who could validate theory in their teaching strategies . . . the teachers in the classrooms'. The report commissioned by Her Majesty's Chief Inspector of Schools on *Teaching of Reading in Inner London Primary Schools* confirms that 'Teachers themselves have to be more knowledgeable and skilled about reading in order to teach it successfully' (Ofsted, 1996, p. 8).

Fourthly, there are many excellent books on the theoretical aspects of literacy, and there are some useful publications on the practice of the teaching of reading and writing, but few books combine both aspects, and rarely is an eclectic approach advocated and a balanced theoretical stance adopted.

This book aims to be both informative and practical in its classroom application. It is intended to support the work of primary headteachers, classteachers and students in training for the early years in primary school, namely, nurseries, reception and Key Stage 1 classes. The book is broadly based on a research project conducted by the author as part of her work as Course Leader of the Primary Postgraduate Certificate of Education at the Institute of Education, University of London. The research project arose from the author's interest in and concern for the teaching of reading which were rooted in her experience of infant teaching, along with experience gained as a member of a local education authority primary advisory service and from lecturing on both primary pre- and in-service courses.

The teaching of reading

The book also draws on the research literature that underpins the suggestions for classroom practice in a way that is intended to be informative and manageable. The belief that informed practice can only develop from a genuine understanding of the literacy process is maintained as the book charts the way in which the young child progresses from the first glimmerings of the purpose and recognition of what text is, to a state of fully developed fluent reading.

The book develops ideas in the following way. Chapter 1, 'The importance of the first year of school', cites research evidence of the long-lasting benefits of a successful first year of school, for which Pedersen *et al.* (1978), Mortimore *et al.* (1988), Tizard *et al.* (1988) and Sammons *et al.* (1995) provide useful longitudinal evidence.

The studies of Aubrey (1993) and Riley (1994) shed further light into processes of teaching and learning, in mathematics and literacy, respectively, in the first year of schooling. The path from emergent literacy to conventional beginning reading (Riley, 1996a) is described and the implications for classroom practice are made explicit.

Chapter 2, 'The process of literacy', proposes a theoretical model for the process of reading and its complexity. There is acknowledgement of the need to balance the contribution of both meaning emphasis and code emphasis theories in order to achieve a comprehensive explanation of how children learn to read.

Discussion about the links between writing and reading makes a wider consideration of literacy development both necessary and theoretically sound, rather than a sole focus on reading development. Suggestions are made regarding approaches to the teaching of reading so that all the inter-related aspects of literacy development are supported.

Chapter 3, 'Four case studies', describes the work of four reception classteachers and their classes of children with very similar entry skill scores. Two of the classes made strikingly greater progress than the other two. The reasons for this are offered, plus the implications of highly developed diagnostic skills on the part of the teacher. Suggestions for practice are made – namely, the monitoring of progress and teaching to support the development of useful reading strategies.

Chapter 4, 'Positive school adjustment and success with reading', is a discussion of the need for positive adjustment to school in order that children learn effectively. The research evidence cited is now over twenty years old and relatively dated. The work comes from Ilg and Ames (1965), Johannsen (1965), Austin and Lafferty (1968) and Thompson (1975).

The research findings from the project carried out by the author are reported to show that those children who did not settle well, and therefore had not adjusted to school easily, for whatever reason, were four times less likely to be reading by the end of the first year of school regardless of their entry skills.

Surprisingly, this finding had no relationship with the child's age at school entry. Implications for admission procedures for primary schools and the role and importance of the reception teacher are addressed.

Chapter 5, 'The organisation of a learning environment', gives a summary of the teaching of reading through the reception year and Key Stage 1. The need to match methods and approaches closely to each child's developmental stage is discussed.

The different facets of reading development, i.e. *phonological awareness* (the ability to recognise and manipulate shared sounds in words), *orthographic knowledge* (print processing demonstrated through word recognition and understanding of spelling patterns) and the use of *context* and *syntax* (grammar) in decoding ability all need to be supported through a variety of teaching approaches in very specific ways. The teaching of reading in the early years of school is addressed within a balanced literacy programme. Suggestions are made regarding effective ways of grouping children and organising their learning in a classroom situation in order to achieve effective literacy teaching.

As already noted, this book is broadly based on a research project, which was divided into two parts.

Part 1 focused on the children, and the aims of the study were achieved by:

- assessing the range of literacy development exhibited by 191 children on entry to school; and
- identifying the entry skills that most reliably predict success in reading by the end of the first year of school.

Part 2 focused on the reception teachers and the aims were achieved by considering the extent to which reception teachers facilitate a mastery of literacy by both capitalising on, and teaching to, each pupil's prior knowledge and understanding of literacy.

Part 1 of the study

During the two-year project, 191 children were assessed, each September soon after school entry. The different aspects of functioning that were measured were

- general maturity and intellectual functioning
- literacy-related skills
- adjustment to school.

At the end of the year, in July, two aspects of the children's functioning were assessed:

- General maturity and cognitive functioning.
- Written and spoken language.

Full details of the measures used can be found in Appendix 2. Thirty-two classes were studied in 16 primary schools from rural, surburban and inner-city local education authorities. The data were analysed using both descriptive and parametric statistical techniques. The main findings are as follows:

- Children arrive at school with a possible range of five years in their functioning regarding literacy-related skills and intellectual ability.
- Pearson's correlations, multiple regression and discriminant analyses confirm that the ability to identify letters of the alphabet and write one's name at school entry are the most powerful predictors of successful reading by the end of the year. This confirms the importance attached to these abilities in the findings of earlier studies (Wells and Raban, 1978; Tizard *et al.*, 1988).
- Understanding of the communicative function and the conventions of print, although weaker, has a positive relationship with reading.
- An explanation of these data is that there is a developmental pathway to fluent reading. The child develops through the emergent literacy phase, with the accretion of an understanding of print and text through to the phase of beginning conventional reading. Progression takes place through the transition phase of whole word processing, Frith's (1985) logographic stage, to the alphabetic stage into conventional reading. Arriving at school able to identify the letters of the alphabet and being able to write one's name indicates a more refined processing of print is needed for this transition phase.
- Children who do not adjust to school are four times less likely to be able to read by the end of their first year in school.

Part 2 of the study

A sample of reception classteachers was investigated through a postal questionnaire survey. The questionnaire examined

- the extent to which reception classteachers are aware of the most predictive entry skills;
- the ability of reception classteachers to identify the skills in their new school entrants; and
- the use that reception classteachers made in their teaching of reading of the most valuable entry skills with which children arrive at school.

Teachers involved with Part 1 of the study were recruited, and an additional group in a wide geographical area were circulated with the postal questionnaire. The main findings from these data showed that

- the majority of the reception classteachers surveyed ranked the importance of the entry skills in the reverse order to those found to be most valuable in Part 1 of the study; and
- reception classteachers use approaches to reading that develop understandings of print and its usefulness. They foster the enjoyment of books. However, they do not appear to value the importance of orthographic (print-processing) awareness, as demonstrated by the ability to identify and label the letters of the alphabet in the child's repertoire of strengths at school entry. Therefore, the teachers are ill-placed to match their teaching closely to the child's existing knowledge.

The main finding and, consequently, the recurring theme of this book, is that the new school entrant is very competent and due, presumably, to insufficient awareness, reception classteachers are unable to capitalise fully on the child's prior but highly idiosyncratic knowledge.

The view promoted in this book concerning the way literacy is developed is encapsulated by Clay (1991, p. 1), when she writes:

> A theory emerges which hypothesizes that out of early reading and writing experiences the young learner creates a network of competencies which power subsequent independent literacy learning. It is the theory of generic learning, that is, learning which generates further learning. The generic competencies are constructed by the learner as he works on many kinds of information coming from the printed page in reading or going from the printed page in writing.

In addition to this theory of learning, the book draws extensively on recent research findings (from the field of experimental and educational psychology with special scrutiny of the findings from the project carried out by the author) that inform the classroom practitioner about both the reading process and the ways in which literacy development can be most effectively supported.

When the vast majority of the adult population in our society could not read, the small minority who were literate gained membership of an exclusive club through which access to unimagined horizons became possible. Ideas generated were shared, challenged, developed and extended. Today, children who cannot read are denied entry to a club and, whilst its exclusivity may be diminished, they are nevertheless denied access to education, culture, power and importance. This book addresses itself to those working in primary schools with the youngest children in the hope of reducing the number of individuals who are kept on the doorstep outside the club.

1

The Importance of the First Year
of School

---

*... don't you know that in every task the most important thing is the
beginning, and especially when you deal with anything young and tender.*
(Plato)

Political and educational interest was focused on the early years of
school by the report of the National Commission for Education
(1995). One of the report's main recommendations (pp. 2 and 15)
was that 'All children must achieve a good grasp of literacy and
basic skills early on as the foundation for learning throughout life
... investment of taxpayer's money in increased support for children aged 3–8 years was needed'. This chapter reaffirms the commission's conviction of the importance of the early years of
mainstream school in the light of research findings. It is now becoming clear that it is in the first few months of school that effective learning patterns are established, and that they set the scene
for future educational success, with a special emphasis on an early
and successful start with reading and writing.

Setting the scene

First, the work of cognitive psychologists over the last decade has
repeatedly shown the extraordinary ability of young children to
make sense of the world and to learn. For example, Gordon Wells's
work demonstrated the child's extensive capacity to acquire spoken language, to achieve a vocabulary of at least 6,000 or 7,000
words before starting school and to attain most of the vagaries of a
complex grammar system. Also, Martin Hughes's work explored
the young child's grasp of the symbolic representation of a number
system. Accumulating evidence from Tizard and Hughes (1984),
Wells (1985a, b) and Hughes (1986) led Donaldson (1989, p. 36) to

write 'that children are highly active and efficient learners, competent enquirers, eager to understand'. Given this natural propensity,
it would seem logical that, once the new school entrant enters the
reception class, the teacher should harness this great potential as
quickly and effectively as possible.

Secondly, there is convincing longitudinal evidence to support
the long-term benefit of an effective early start to mainsteam
school. The earliest study to point to the fact that the first year of
school may be of special importance is from the USA and is
nearly twenty years old (Pedersen *et al.*, 1978). These researchers
found that a group of children who had been taught by a particular first-grade teacher, 'Miss A', seemed to have been given an
initial boost to their education that provided an advantage
throughout the remainder of their schooling. The research methodology was an unusual and retrospective one. The researchers
used the school annual report cards to track the academic progress of the groups of children in Miss A's school (i.e. over many
years, the annual scores of all the classes from entry in elementary
school to exit from secondary school). It seemed that this excep-
tional teacher achieved results with her pupils in early literacy
and numeracy far beyond those of her colleagues with parallel
intakes.

When the researchers interviewed the pupils who had been
taught by Miss A some twenty years later, three-quarters of them
rated her as a very good or excellent teacher, whilst they could
remember nothing about their other elementary schoolteachers. It
was said that 'it did not matter what background or abilities the
beginning pupil had; there was no way that the pupil was not
going to read by the end of grade one' (cited in Pedersen *et al.*,
1978, p. 19). Miss A left no child unaware of the importance of
schooling and the personal effort it required to make use of the
opportunities it offered. She herself stayed late working with slow-
learning pupils, sharing her lunch with children who had none and
teaching with dedication, application and 'a lot of love!', in the
words of a former colleague (*ibid.*, p. 20).

More recent evidence comes from the findings of the Infant
School Study (Tizard *et al.*, 1988). This project followed a cohort of
children in 33 inner London schools from the end of the nursery
class to the end of infant school. The main aim was to investigate
the progress of children in order to explain the reasons for their
differing rates of attainment. Learning and teaching are hugely

complex and, when variables such as home background, ethnic origin and factors both within the school and *between* teachers are also explored, and their varying influences accounted for in the analyses, it becomes a challenge in itself to explain the relationships between the different variables. For the purpose of this discussion the most important finding is that it was only in the reception year that certain classes made greater rates of progress than others. When analysed these rates were found to be statistically significant. Furthermore, the Tizard project showed that those children who had made the greatest amount of progress in the reception class remained the highest achievers all through infant school.

Regarding the teaching and learning processes investigated, Tizard (1993) writes that the children whose teachers had high expectations of their progress were often children whom they considered a 'pleasure to teach' and who would be introduced to a wider curriculum than the children who had similar skills at the beginning of the year, but whom they did not expect to do so well.

As Tizard (1993, p. 77) says: 'We had evidence that the reception year has a particularly large effect on progress. The correlations [relationships] between the children's scores at the beginning and end of the reception year were a good deal lower than in subsequent years'. In other words, the lower correlation (or the weaker relationship between the scores at the beginning and end of the year) signifies greater progress made in the first year that might be attributed to effective teaching. A table of the Pearson correlations is given in Appendix I. Tizard *et al.* (1988) followed up part of the sample of the children at the end of their primary school (at 11 years of age), and the rank order of the children's scores had not changed. According to this study, over a period of seven years of primary school, an early positive start appears to be important.

Another influential study – the Junior School Project (Mortimore *et al.*, 1988) – corroborates this research finding. This equally ambitious and complex project explored the organisation and the teaching and learning processes of the four junior years (Years 3, 4, 5 and 6 in post-National Curriculum terminology). Amongst many other important findings, Mortimore *et al.* found that the rank order of children's test scores remained constant over the four years. In other words, how well the children were doing at the start of junior school powerfully predicted how well they would be

doing at 11 years of age. Once again this points to the value of a
successful start to schooling. The children were also followed to
the end of secondary school (Sammons *et al.*, 1994). Those pupils
who had been the highest achievers at the end of primary school
were those who gained the best GCSE results. Schools and individual classteachers *do* make a difference to children's academic progress; and an effective start appears to be especially important for
academic success throughout infant, junior and secondary school.

It would seem, then, from these longitudinal projects that the
reception year and certain highly skilled reception classteachers
have great influence on children's learning. An explanation as to
why the first year should be quite so important has begun to
emerge. Two studies exploring the teaching and learning processes
in the reception year of school complement each other in a way
that adds to understanding. Aubrey (1993) and Riley (1994) point
to the fact that the new pupil brings a rich store of knowledge and
skills to the task of learning mathematics (Aubrey) and acquiring
literacy (Riley, 1995a) in school. Children have learned a great deal
through their experience of living in a world in which a number
rule system operates and where they are surrounded by print; both
studies show that the challenge to the reception teacher is to be
able to identify the child's abilities and understanding in order to
facilitate progress.

As Aubrey (1993, p. 39) writes:

> Whilst they may not possess the formal conventions for represent-
> ing it, reception age children clearly enter school having acquired
> already much mathematical content. In terms of specific teaching
> implications as in early reading stages, in early stages of learning
> mathematics, perhaps too children should be prompted to extend
> the range of strategies at their disposal so that their natural invent-
> iveness is not undermined by a struggle to find the one single,
> convergent and acceptable response.

Similar results were found in literacy development by Riley
(1995a) – a wide range of development exists at school entry. Some
children were functioning at the level of a 3-year-old with only the
haziest understanding of how books and print work, whilst other
pupils were well on the road to beginning reading. Some of the
teachers were aware of the differences in their new entrants and
sought to devise reading programmes that facilitated development
precisely. Other reception classteachers used a 'scatter gun' approach, randomly trying a variety of methods in the hope that

'something must work'. Most worryingly, the majority of reception teachers appear from their questionnaire responses to rank order the important literacy-related entry skills in the reverse order to those found by the research project to be the most powerful predictors of later reading. This is clearly an example of thinking and belief systems based on an ill-founded ideology that is adversely affecting teaching practices (Beard and Oakhill, 1994). There is an important, new message emanating from the author's research findings which will be expanded later.

The new school entrant has acquired a store of knowledge but this is highly idiosyncratic. Much confusion can be caused by inappropriate teaching that cuts across this prior learning; alternatively, development can be effectively fostered with skilful support. This principle of 'scaffolding' the child into a higher level of functioning was suggested by Bruner when he elaborated upon Vygotsky's notion of the individual's 'zone of proximal development'. This research finding, which is of crucial importance for the reception and Key Stage 1 classteacher, also offers an explanation for the reported benefit of smaller class sizes in the early years of school (Word *et al.*, 1990). This mode of teaching (with the adult as diagnostician) makes the issue of class size unavoidable. It has to be accepted that young children, at this stage of development, need to be taught in small groups or as individuals in order to effect the greatest progress.

An additional reason why lower numbers in classes are so vital in the early years is that greater numbers of pupils in a reception class will affect the teacher's capacity to settle the children as they make the transition from home or nursery to school. That children have to be happy and feel secure in order to learn is widely acknowledged. Cleave *et al.* (1982) and Bennett and Kell (1989) relate horror stories of young children, sobbing and bewildered, in the early weeks of school. Riley (1995b) found that those children who did not adjust positively and quickly to school after the first half-term, as judged by their teachers, were four times less likely to be reading by the end of the year – whatever their skills on entry. This notion will be expanded and its implications discussed in Chapter 4.

In setting the scene for a book about the teaching of literacy, it is important to recognise the nature of the material with which early-years teachers work. Research evidence suggests that young children are natural and competent learners, and that a successful start can be made by capitalising on their previously acquired knowledge. It is crucial not to waste this early and, for the most part, incidental learning. Children should not be confused or, worse still, alienated by inappropriate teaching experiences. The research findings discussed above uphold the early-years educators' adage of 'observe, support and extend', which needs to be continued throughout the first years of school. In addition to affirming this principle, this book recommends teaching strategies that build on these research insights.

The relationship between reading and success at school

It is well documented that a major contribution to a positive start to school is the child's early success with the task of learning to read. The converse is also true: the implications of poor reading ability are far reaching. Low academic achievement is linked to low reading ability. For over two decades it has been known that reading ability, as measured by reading comprehension, is highly correlated with school performance in diverse subjects (Bloom, 1976; Perfetti, 1976, cited in Daneman, 1991). Reading comprehension is associated with success in many different school subjects. For example, the strong relationship (of the $r = .4$ correlation) between achievement in science and literature approaches zero when the effects of reading comprehension are taken into account (Bloom, 1976).

In addition to providing a means of access to all school subjects, the ability to read promotes a system of thought (Donaldson, 1989). Literacy enables clear, rigorous thought that can both follow and lead an argument – an essential attribute for academic success: 'the thinking itself draws great strength from literacy . . . whenever there is a discussion to develop, whenever there are complex ideas to consider. It is even more obvious that the sustained, orderly communication of this kind of thinking requires considerable mastery of the written word' (Donaldson, 1989, p. 50). Donaldson continues to make the case for 'active and systematic teaching in the furtherance of literacy' (*ibid.*, p. 56) that will encourage quite early 'conscious, reflective ways of considering the written word' (p. 54), and thus empower children in their thinking.

The disadvantages of failing to read early and fluently are also clear. American research findings indicate that those children who do not appear to make sound progress in early reading in their school careers quickly fall behind (Ferreiro and Teberosky, 1982; Stanovich, 1986). It would also appear that schooling does not reduce differences in reading ability, once they occur (Just and Carpenter, 1987, cited in Daneman, 1991). British longitudinal studies (Mortimore *et al.*, 1988; Tizard *et al.*, 1988) also indicate that, once established, the gap between achievers and non-achievers remains or widens throughout primary schooling.

The beginning of reading: a theoretical explanation

The methods of teaching reading in UK primary schools have been the subject of much controversy and debate. It has been reluctantly conceded by educationalists that reading is not as successfully taught as it might be in all reception and Key Stage 1 classes (Gorman and Fernandes, 1992). It is suggested that the main reason for this is that too few primary teachers are sufficiently aware of the research evidence that offers an explanation of the literacy process. Teachers who are in possession of an informed under-standing of the process of literacy and its complexity are in a strong position to provide a structured, multi-approach pro-gramme that supports all the inter-related aspects of print processing.

Emergent literacy

The term 'emergent literacy', first coined by Marie Clay in 1966, has replaced the limbo state of 'prereading' and is used to describe 'the reading and writing behaviours that precede and develop into conventional literacy' (Sulzby, 1989, p. 728). A great deal is now known about the child's competence as he or she begins to under-stand the links between speech and writing, the conventions of print, its unchanging nature and its communicative function. Im-portantly, throughout the 1980s, reading and writing development began increasingly to be viewed as complementary processes of literacy.

Goodman (1980) claims the 'roots of literacy' develop through living in a world of story books, letters, lists and printed materials, and that these experiences are the seed corn of the child's fascination with print. From 6 months to approximately 5 or 6 years of age, the child gradually realises that print has a communicative function (Ferreiro and Teberosky, 1982; Goodman, 1980; 1986). The child comes to understand the purpose of print in a context-rich way: typically, through birthday cards, MacDonald's signs and tooth-paste tubes (McGee *et al.*, 1988, cited in Sulzby and Teale, 1991).

Not surprisingly, sharing story and picture books has received most researchers' attention, as this is the child's main literacy experience prior to mainstream school and the formal task of learning to read. The benefits of reading stories as a socially created, interactive activity (Heath, 1982) are now clear. The young child's independent but not yet conventional readings of books grow out of shared interactive reading with a facilitative adult. These are powerful experiences that advance the child's literacy development (Sulzby, 1989). Wells (1985b; 1988) found a strong positive relationship between story reading and success in reading throughout the primary and secondary school.

Two important features emerge from this body of work. First, the research views the child as an active contributor to his or her own learning. This learner-centred view of the preschool reader and writer has been greatly influenced by Piaget, Bruner and Chomsky. Each of these saw the child as a constructive, hypothesis-testing, rule-generating agent in his or her own learning. Secondly, the studies highlight the role of the supportive, interested, interactive adult, who 'scaffolds' the child into greater understanding. These two crucial aspects of literacy learning have implications for the following phase of development.

The beginnings of conventional reading

Precisely when the reader moves from emergent literacy into beginning conventional reading is arbitrary. Sulzby (1992) defines the transition point as when the child is able to use three aspects of reading in a flexible and co-ordinated way:

- Letter-sound knowledge.
- The concept of a word.
- Comprehension.

Sulzby says that the transition point is blurred, as the child's imperfect understanding regresses and advances through many print encounters before finally moving into conventional print processing.

For a detailed explanation of the developmental path of fluent reading, it is necessary to draw upon experimental psychology to shed light on the young child's print-processing abilities as he or she enters the phase of beginning reading. These have been described by several researchers as phases or stages during which the child processes the print in *qualitatively* different ways.

Ehri (1995) proposes a stage theory of progressively more refined print-processing abilities, described as *prealphabetic, partial alphabetic, full alphabetic* and *consolidated alphabetic.*

Frith's simplifed descriptive stages are useful here for both researchers and practitioners. Frith (1985) describes the phases as follows:

- *The logographic phase* The child reads words as logograms or wholes. The child is supported in word recognition during the emergent literacy phase by distinctive and highly meaningful logos, such as MacDonald's golden arch or Coca-Cola's red label.
- *The alphabetic phase* The child can distinguish individual alphabet letters and begins to apply crude sound/symbol associations. The first and most accessible letters the child recognises are those in his or her own name. These gradually receive wider application in continuous text.
- *The orthographic phase* The more advanced young reader is able to 'chunk' words into orthographic units by sight memory without recourse to phonological conversion. This ability greatly speeds up processing and, as a result, the child is well on the way to fluent reading.

Frith believes that, once the end of this sequence of print-processing ability is complete, integration of strategies results in fluency. The reader has at his or her disposal all the orthographic decoding (processing) skills associated with the three stages and *is able to use all of them.*

A researcher who has made a substantial contribution to the understanding of mechanisms that assist fluent reading development is Goswami (1993), building on the work of Bryant and Bradley (1985). Goswami (1993), like Frith, proposes that there are qualitative differences in children's word processing at the beginning of conventional reading, but she places greater emphasis on phonological awareness and its inter-relatedness with print processing. She writes: 'It may be true, then, to stop thinking of reading development as a series of stages, and to conceive instead of a more interactive developmental process, in which the child's knowledge about the orthography is affected by, and in turn changes, that child's phonological knowledge' (Goswami, 1993, p. 315).

The role of phonological development and, in particular, an awareness of alliteration and rhyme and its power to assist children to learn the connections between letters and sounds, has been a fruitful research interest of Goswami. Her work has shed light on the way the child learns *phonemic segmentation* in the early stages of beginning conventional reading. This crucial skill is the ability to hear the constituent sounds in words and then to map a sound on to a graphic symbol. This skill is developed by reading, but it is also a prerequisite for achieving the alphabetic phase of reading development. Goswami maintains that young children are helped in their aquisition of this skill by the use of spelling-sound patterns of known words, e.g. *beak* to work out the spelling-sound pattern of a new word – *peak*.

It is important to note that children will use the 'rime' or the end of the word (*pink–wink*) to make the analogy rather than the 'onset' or the beginning of the word (*beak–bean*). Goswami suggests that children find the rime easier because it is the first analogy to develop. Even some 3- and 4-year-old preschool children are able to identify words that rhyme, and this ability has a clear-cut connection with later reading progress (e.g. Bradley and Bryant, 1983). It is also proposed that the ability to detect onset and rime is a very useful skill for young readers to acquire because of the greater phonic regularity and consistency of rimes as opposed to other, smaller phonemic units in the English language. This work has direct, valuable implications for the teaching of reading and will be referred to in the suggestions for practice.

It is clear from the above that the developing reader learns to process print in increasingly refined and efficient ways. In addition, the child is using to greater advantage the different strategies available from the text, namely, *contextual*, *semantic* and *syntactic* cues, as well as *orthographic* and *phonological* understanding. Clay (1991) calls this integration the 'construction of inner control' through which the child draws on all his or her understandings and skills to become an independent, fluent reader. Clearly, a cognitive skill of this complexity has to be taught with a full recognition of its multifaceted nature. The implications of this message are addressed in the following five chapters of this book.

The transition from 'emergent literacy' to the beginning of conventional reading: the research findings

A study of literacy development that followed 191 reception children through the first year of school has shed some light on the way the child comes to grips with the complexity of reading and how teachers can gain insight into the print-processing abilities of new pupils (Riley, 1994; 1995a; 1996). This research provides evidence of the value of the young reader's refined orthographic knowledge as indicated by the child's ability both to identify and label letters of the alphabet and to write his or her own name before formal instruction at school begins.

The most significant finding is the relationship between literacy-related skills assessed at school entry and reading (as measured by the raw score of the Neale's Analysis of Reading Test) at the end of the first year of school. (Full details of the assessments used and the statistical analyses carried out are to be found in Appendixes II and III.)

The three literacy-related skills (concepts about print, ability to write his or her own name and the ability to identify and label the letters of the alphabet) assessed by the researchers in September were all shown to be positively related to the ability to read the following July. But by far the most powerful predictor of later success in reading was the child's knowledge of the alphabet, acquired incidentally and informally preschool.

This work adds considerable weight to the body of evidence that recognises that speedy word processing is essential for progress in reading, the first stage of which is an understanding of the alphabet system. A recognition of individual letters and an ability to hear the sounds in words are the first steps in the development of the orthographic and phonological processing capability essential in literacy.

The predictive value of knowing the alphabet and the child's ability to write his or her own name are not new findings: they reaffirm the views of Wells and Raban (1978) and the findings of the Infant School Study (Tizard *et al.*, 1988) regarding the strength of the association of orthographic knowledge with later reading. What is perhaps less fully appreciated is what these findings mean about the child's orthographic knowledge, as indicated by the continued influence of concepts about print in the statistical analyses.

The importance of orthographic knowledge

The studies that followed up the early finding, some thirty years ago (Bond and Dykstra, 1967; Chall, 1967), of the connection between knowledge of letters of the alphabet and early reading development were disappointing in the extreme. When Gibson and Levin (1975) and Ehri (1983) set out to teach children the letters of the alphabet directly, prior to school entry, there appeared to be no positive link with successful later reading.

Blatchford *et al.* (1987) argue in their Infant School Study that the strong relationship found between letter knowledge on school entry and later reading probably reflects children's prior and more general acquaintance with written language. This is at odds with Smith's (1973) assertion that skilful readers do not process individual letters, and from which he deduced that beginners do not need this ability in order to be able to read fluently. This seems to be the main tenet of Smith's theory, to which many teachers adhere and which is strongly reflected in their teaching. It is useful to consider this assertion critically in the light of psychological evidence.

It is not that an experienced reader decodes letter by letter. In explaining the function of eye fixations in the fluent reader in order to process print, Adams (1991, p. 22) writes:

> showing admirable adaptivity, then, readers tend to center their gaze toward the middle of words, taking a second fix to the right when the word is so long as to require it (Rayner and Pollatsek, 1987). To the extent that any sequence in view is familiar, its component letters pull each other into familiar words and patterns by virtue of the learned associations among them. Because this happens automatically and in the course of perception, the letters are processed neither independently nor serially. Instead their recognition is highly interdependent and happens more or less in parallel.

An ability to recognise and label letters is the first step towards this automaticity.

The failure of such research projects as Gibson and Levin (1975) and Ehri (1983a) to establish a connection between *teaching* the alphabet to preschoolers and later success with reading seems to suggest that this skill has to be acquired in a more 'hard won' and 'incidental' manner through long-term exposure to books and environmental print in the emergent, preschool literacy phase.

The emerging literate child moves from conceptual to formal to symbolic levels of understanding letters. The symbolic relationship between letters and sounds is the basis of the English writing system. Vygotsky (1978, p. 106) states: 'A feature of this [writing] system is that it is second order symbolism, which gradually becomes direct symbolism'. This means that written language consists of a system of signs that designate the sounds and words of spoken language, which, in turn are signs for real entities and relations. Bialystok (1991) conducted a study that explored this gradual shift in understanding of children between 3 and 5 years of age. She designed labelling and spelling tasks using plastic letters. Of all the instruments, her 'moving word' task proved to be the most powerful predictor of success. Through this, she concluded that the child's most essential insight is the symbolic relation by which letters represent sounds. This clearly needs to be exploited in school, and the early awareness of letter/sound correspondence developed into a gradual appreciation of the English alphabetic system and its complexities.

Bialystok (*ibid.*, p. 78) writes:

> Children's first achievement with letters is as part of a procedure, namely reciting the alphabet . . . Reading requires symbolic knowledge of letters. The representation must include the relation between the letter and its sound. Objects *have* meanings; symbols represent meanings. Objects can *make* sounds; symbols *stand for* sounds. Meaning is somehow *in* objects; it is not in symbols. For this reason formal knowledge of the alphabet is not sufficient for learning to read.

This explains why merely teaching the alphabet has no enduring value and fails to guarantee an early successful start to reading. The appreciation of the symbolic representation of letters for spoken sounds occurs slowly over time and with exposure to meaningful experiences of print and text.

In the experimental group, those children who could read were more successful in all the word tasks undertaken, they were of the same age and there was no significant difference between their receptive vocabulary scores from the non-readers in the study. Bialystok (*ibid.*, p. 87) suggests that 'the difference between those children who could read and those who could not has something to do with the way in which they understand the letter-sound correspondences'. The child's knowledge of language gives him or her access to the symbolic system.

Knowing letter names *or* sounds on entry to school indicates experience with print, cognitive and perceptual maturity and the requisite attention span, in addition to a symbolic understanding of the alphabet. Downing (1979) provides a 'cognitive clarity' model which leads to a clearer and clearer appreciation of the alphabetic system. He asserts that superior letter-name knowledge is a symptom of a greater understanding of the technical features of writing and is one of the prerequisite concepts for fluent reading. Together they are the concepts

- that the continuous flow of speech can be segmented into parts;
- of the spoken word;
- of the phoneme;
- of code – that an abstract symbol can represent something else;
- of the written word;
- of the grapheme; and
- of the letter.

Bialystok's study provides insight into different levels of ability to identify letters. These levels denote more advanced understandings of words and the symbolic nature of language. The child who has learned to identify his or her letters, incidentally as it were over time and through many meaningful encounters with print, has developed a deeper, more sophisticated appreciation of the role of letters in the representation of sounds. The child in possession of this understanding at school entry is further along the road to reading than the child who is merely able to recite the alphabet.

Adams (1993, p. 207) hints at the transition phase of reading development when she writes:

> For children who, on entering the classroom, do not yet have a comfortable familiarity with the letters of the alphabet, finding ways to help them is of first order importance. Even so, knowledge of letters is of little value unless the *child knows and is interested in their use.* Correctly perceived and interpreted, print conveys information. In keeping with this, children's concepts about print are also strong predictors of the ease with which they will learn to read. Before formal instruction is begun, children should possess a broad and general appreciation of the nature of print.

Implications for practice

Fisher (1992, p. 36) says:

> children starting school are already successful and active learners who bring considerable knowledge and experience to the task of literacy learning. Children learn best when they are able to relate what they are doing to their own experience. They also learn most successfully when the learning takes place within a social context, particularily from interaction with a caring adult or more experienced child. Home is a good place to learn and, although homes vary, there is much to be learned from the way the child has learned in the home.

The essential role of assessment at school entry

As the earlier discussion has revealed, teachers who work with young children need to be skilled, diagnostic facilitators of their pupils' early literacy attempts. At best children mimic the role of adults who, preschool, so powerfully assisted in much valuable literacy progress. Sadly, at worst, nursery and reception classteachers cut across the child's rich, but highly idiosyncratic, prior learning to confuse and dishearten (Baker and Raban, 1991).

Precisely when the initial assessment occurs is a decision for each school to make, depending on their admission policies and mode of organisation. Many schools consider that it is more useful to allow children to settle for half a term before recording their levels of development. However, the increasing need for 'baseline assessment' makes the timing of this assessment close to the child's arrival at school a necessity. The information gathered at school entry enables meaningful comparison with attainment, as measured by the Standard Assessment Tasks at the end of Key Stage 1. Increasing accountability is required of schools, and evidence of effective teaching is sought by inspectors and governing bodies. However, the main purpose of assessing the pupil on arrival at school is to provide valuable insight into the child's abilities and understandings in order to inform teaching usefully.

Information the classteacher needs to record

General information on the child

Some of this information will be noted at school entry and updated as appropriate and with evidence of progress:

- Relevant admission data including number of siblings, place in the family, etc. (This is especially important for bilingual children whose parents are not fluent English speakers. The school needs to know if there are older English-speaking siblings who can help with literacy.)
- Preschool experience.
- Relevant information after discussion with parents or carers including their concerns and expectations.
- Medical information regarding hearing, sight and general health.
- General physical and social development.
- Evidence of the level of the child's self-esteem and confidence.
- Ability to dress him or herself, go to the toilet, etc.
- Evidence of child's ability to integrate with his or her peers and cope with the class/school setting.

Aspects of the child's intellectual functioning

- Information gathered from observing the child at play in structured and unstructured activities.
- Ability to concentrate for periods of time on a task.

- The child's ability to represent the world and him or herself (i.e. draw him or herself).
- Colours known.
- Numbers known (are letters and numbers confused?).
- Nursery rhymes known.

Assessment of the child's spoken language

- Whether English is the first or additional language (if English is the second language, what is the home language?).
- The level of confidence when communicating with adults or peers.
- The ability to respond to questions, directions and requests.
- Ability to communicate needs, ideas and feelings.

Assessment of the child's understanding of written language, its purpose and conventions

Concepts about print

- Demonstrates an awareness that signs and labels communicate a message (i.e. show awareness of pupils' name labels, labels on boxes and equipment, signs in the home corner, etc.).
- When sharing a book indicates understanding
  - that the story starts at the front of the book;
  - of the terms 'front' and 'back';
  - that the print (not pictures) tells the story;
  - where the print starts, and which way it goes;
  - of the convention of the 'sweep back' (i.e. the place of the next word at the end of a line);
  - of the meta-language of print – word/letter/sentence/full stop; and
  - that, within a word, there are individual letters.

Orthographic awareness

- Number of letters (by either name or sound, upper or lower case) of the alphabet that can be identified.
- Ability to express him or herself with any written marks in order to communicate.

Phonological awareness

The ability to
- hear *very* distinctly different words, i.e. 'sat/chat/fat/Jane';

- detect words that rhyme from non-rhyming words, i.e. m-*at*/h-*at*/ c-*at*/r-*ap*; and
- detect words with the same onset, e.g. *m*-an/*m*-at/*m*-ap/*c*-an.

Positive attitudes to books and literacy

- Voluntarily looking at books with enjoyment.
- Writing notes, messages and stories spontaneously.
- Enjoys hearing stories read.
- Valuing and caring for books.

These suggestions for observations provide evidence of the child's specific needs regarding language development. In addition, these assessments will enable the reception teacher to provide appropriate teaching and to inform others in the school.

2

The Process of Literacy

As [the reader] brings the text to life, he casts back and forth in his head for connections between what he is reading and what he already knows. His eyes scan forward or jump backwards. He pauses, rushes on, selects from his memory whatever relates the meaning to his experience or his earlier reading, in a rich and complex system of to-ing and fro-ing in his head, storing, reworking, understanding or being puzzled.

(Meek, 1982, p. 21)

Teachers who understand the complexity of how children learn to read are in a much better position to provide a structured, multiapproach programme that supports all the aspects of print processing necessary for fluent reading to be developed in the first years of school. This chapter considers the process of literacy in terms of its constituent parts and the way it operates as a whole. An understanding of this inter-relationship is crucial for the classroom practitioner to achieve maximum progress with pupils.

A model of the reading process

The teaching of literacy is fraught with mythology, opinion and polarised positions. The respective roles of 'meaning' and 'code-breaking' strategies are seen by various theorists as having different emphases in the child's developing competence. That models of the reading process differ and are partisan is hardly surprising. Two of the dominant models directly oppose each other. 'Bottom-up' theories propose a subskills approach, which suggests that reading is learned initially by manipulating the smallest units of language (i.e. letters, words). The reverse position is taken by theories commonly referred to as 'top down'. These theories suggest that the search for meaning is central from the outset, and that the main strategies for decoding words are prediction and guessing (Smith, 1971; 1978; Goodman, 1976; Goodman and Goodman, 1979).

These two theoretical positions have greatly influenced how reading is taught. In the USA, the viewpoints are vigorously debated, and expressed as 'phonics and direct instruction' versus 'whole language'. On the surface the discussion is about teaching methods, but the deeper level of disagreement is about what it is that children have to learn in order to be able to read. A number of fundamental questions are central to this issue.

First, which aspect of language plays the most important part in learning to read? Are syntax and semantics the most crucial, or is phonology? The second issue is one of naturalness. How far can learning to read and write be seen as an extension of speaking and listening, or does the child's previous experience of spoken language actually make the acquisition of literacy more difficult?

Adams (1991), in a paper entitled 'Why not phonics and whole language?', comments that the 'whole language' approach, as it is used in the USA, is very difficult to define. It is founded on a view of the reading process that is based on assumptions about

- child-centred instruction;
- the integration of reading and writing;
- a disavowal of the value of teaching or learning of phonics; and
- the view that children are naturally predisposed towards written language acquisition.

However, polarised positions typically create more heat than light. As Elliott (1992, p. 17) writes, in response to the debate initiated by Martin Turner in 1991 when he raised the issue of falling standards of literacy, 'If any single approach to the teaching of reading had unequivocally demonstrated a superiority to other methods, the current controversy would long since be resolved'.

Issues of pedagogy emanate from an understanding of the reading process. The 'Great Debate' (a term coined by Chall, 1967) states the two philosophical positions are in essence ones of 'naturalness' and 'unnaturalness'. Reid (1993, p. 23) summarises the 'natural' position very succinctly. The main assumptions of this position seem to be as follows:

1) The spoken language draws on a special kind of innate ability. For normal children teaching is not necessary. The ability seems relatively independent of intelligence. Children discover for themselves how language works, and the learning can thus be described as 'natural'.

2) Reading is the exact parallel to listening, only in the visual mode. The special learning ability will also work for reading as children are exposed to written language and given clues about meaning. Thus learning to read is also 'natural'.

3) The systematic teaching of letter-sound correspondences is a distracting interference with those 'natural' learning processes, in that it fragments a process that must remain 'whole'.

4) The key to fluent reading is not word recognition but the use of strategies such as forming 'hypotheses', predicting (also called guessing/expecting/anticipating) and the selecting of maximally *productive* cues to confirm meaning. Those strategies are also the basis of the skilled comprehension of speech. The text as constituted by the reader may not correspond exactly to what is on the page.

These assumptions are present in one form or another in the early writings of Smith (1971) and Goodman (1972, as cited in Donaldson, 1989). Goodman (1972, cited in Donaldson, 1989, p. 38) writes optimistically that if only teachers would take heed of his work 'it is entirely possible that within the next decade virtually all children will be learning to read, easily and effectively'. This belief has led to the 'minimal teaching movement' (Donaldson, 1989). It has also led to the 'whole language movement' in the USA and to the teaching of reading through 'real books' in the UK. This last, misleading, term was first used in the early 1980s and referred to story books written for children. 'Real books' were analogous to 'real ale' or 'real food'. The term was coined in antithesis to books written for a published, structured reading scheme. The 'real books' or 'apprenticeship approach' was promoted through the booklet, *Read with Me* (Waterland, 1985).

As Beard and Oakhill (1994) note in their critique of the 'apprenticeship approach', whilst every researcher, theorist and practitioner of the teaching of literacy applauds the premise that learning to read should be fun and made so by the sharing of attractive children's books, the apprenticeship approach is only *one* approach regarding 'the bridges between spoken and written language' (Donaldson, 1989; Reid, 1993). A teaching programme also needs to take into account the complexity of the literacy process.

Clem (1990) shows clearly the extreme positions taken on the teaching of reading (see Figures 2.1 and 2.2). The child's attention is drawn to linking sounds with their letter forms, through code emphasis approaches which characteristically focus first on the smallest unit. By contrast, in the meaning emphasis approach, the child is encouraged to focus on the larger units of language, stressing the importance of context and content.

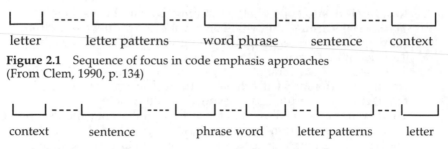

Figure 2.1 Sequence of focus in code emphasis approaches
(From Clem, 1990, p. 134)

Figure 2.2 Sequence of focus in meaning emphasis approaches
(From Clem, 1990, p. 134)

The meaning emphasis proponents are usually high on rhetoric and weaker on classroom practice. The main difference between the two approaches seems to lie in the perception of the experienced and beginning reader's skills. As Clem (1990, p. 136) asserts, the basic tenets underlying 'whole language' reading fail to provide instruction in the tasks at the very beginning of conventional reading, the stage on which this book focuses:

> the exclusive initial focus on context and meaning [withholds] even causal attention to letter/sound units until the students are totally immersed in the print medium. The assumption that all emerging readers can independently meet the challenges of metalinguistic awareness, segmentation, association – the very foundations of automacity and skilled reading – is the fundamental weakness of the 'whole language' position.

This need not and *should not* advocate a return to dry, uncontextualised phonics programmes but a combination of *both* approaches (Adams, 1990). Reading, it is now recognised, is a combination of 'bottom-up' and 'top-down' processes, particularly in the early stages. This is acknowledged by many specialists in the field, including Frith (1980), Marsh *et al.* (1980), Adams (1990), Beard (1990) and Dombey *et al.* (1991). *The Balance Manifesto* (1991) is a call for balance in the teaching of literacy and language skills signed by teachers, academics and writers concerned about the negative nature of the many assertions put forward in the reading debate over the last few years (Stainthorp, 1992).

Merritt (1985) affirms that word recognition and comprehension are the two reasonable starting points for a teacher seeking to develop reading skills. Insight has been gained from experimental research into the process of literacy and the necessity to develop the complementary skills. It is the purpose of this book to promote an *interactive* model of the process of reading – a model that represents a combination of both 'top-down' and 'bottom-up' approaches. (For further reading on the theoretical aspect of literacy, see Bielby, 1994.)

The interactive model

A comprehensive method of teaching reading needs to draw on an explanation of the literacy process that accounts for its complexity. Figure 2.3 reaffirms the inter-relatedness of the different processes involved. The visual stimuli of the print (orthography) are processed in conjunction with the sound units of speech (phonology) they represent. The stimulation has three-way processing, each aspect informing and clarifying the other as it feeds into the meaning and context processors. Meaning provides the dynamo for the whole activity of reading, giving it purpose. To support all the inter-related aspects of the literacy process, systematic teaching is essential. Donaldson (1989) writes: 'The different strands should combine in different ways at different times.'

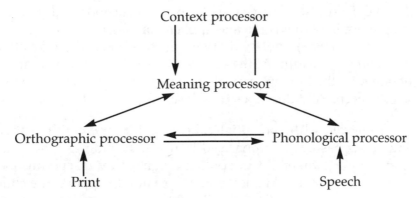

Figure 2.3 The inter-relatedness of the reading process (From Adams, 1990, p. 158)

Understandings and skills that contribute to the literacy process

Spoken language

There is a direct connection between decoding symbols that represent spoken language and knowledge of spoken language (meta-language) (Clark, 1976). The level of linguistic awareness is at a surface and at a deep structure level. Through this language acquisition and attention to meaning, structure is nevertheless learnt. An awareness of the phonological and grammatical features of language are necessary before reading and writing can be achieved.

As Adams (1990, pp. 294–5) says:

> For purposes of learning to read and write, however, these sub-units must be dug out of their normal, sub-attentional status. Children must push their attention down from the level of comprehension at which it normally works. Not surprisingly the deeper into the system they push the harder it is to do. Thus awareness of clauses or prepositions develops earlier and more easily than awareness of words. Awareness of words develops earlier and more easily than the awareness of syllables. An awareness of syllables develops earlier and more easily than the awareness of phonemes.

As the child attends school his or her language develops (Clay, 1991) and the child learns to broaden his or her use of spoken language to accommodate new registers and functions with different individuals in a variety of situations. Meanings become more precise and richer, vocabulary widens and sentence patterns become more complex. The child also becomes aware of constructions and conventions present in both written and spoken language.

Donaldson (1989) and Reid (1993) make explicit the ways that the teaching of reading skills can capitalise, in the early years of schooling, on the human learning that has occurred in the acquisition of speech. Reid describes these as bridges or links:

- *Shared reading*   The potential value of adults and children sharing books has been emphasised in research findings. The adult first supports the child in spoken language by discussing pictures and the story. At a later stage, the adult supports the child in his or her growing familiarity with the conventions of print and book language. Shared reading is currently formalised into reading programmes in primary schools. Adults share books at home, and opportunities should exist for books to be shared in school as frequently as possible.
- *Helping children to produce written language*   Adults can help children to be part of the writing process by collaborating in the encoding of speech – by writing for children and making books with them. The use of commercially produced materials to facilitate writing, as described by Mackay *et al.* (1970), can also

be of great value. Selecting and forming prewritten words into sentences short-circuits the very young child's grapho-motor abilities to make the link from thought to speech to print easier.

- *Use of print embedded in the environment*   Children in the 'logographic' stage of reading development are able, for example, to recognise MacDonald's and Weetabix logos in a print-filled environment. Reid suggests that teaching in schools should capitalise on this developing skill. Schools should use print in an embedded form to maximum advantage, in the same way it has been used so valuably for children in the 'emergent literacy' stage. Meaningful use should be made of labels on packaging, notices in public places and wall displays in school.

These approaches to the teaching of reading are expanded in Chapter 5. The different aspects of the literacy process will now be considered.

Understanding the literacy task

Children who learn to read and write early and easily (some before they start school) have one thing in common: they are knowledge-able about and understand the communicative function of the written word (Durkin, 1966; Clark, 1976). In contrast, Vygotsky (1962) commented on children's vague ideas about the usefulness of reading on entry to school. Downing (1979) found this vague-ness to be widespread across different countries and cultures. Reid's went some way to clarify the early confusions children have that hinder their progress in reading. Downing (1979) and Clay (1985) further researched the misconceptions young readers have about print and its purpose.

A useful list of the understandings of print that gradually de-velop through the 'emergent literacy' phase is provided by Hall (1987, pp. 32–3):

Children learn that:

- when we read we rely on print to carry the message;
- we read and use books in a particular order – from front to back;
- we follow the print in a certain order: line by line, word by word;
- books and print have a particular orientation;
- print is made up of letters, words, punctuation and spaces;
- There are relationships between words spoken and the print observed;
- print is different from pictures;
- there is a language associated with the activity of reading books: front, back, page, word, letter, etc.

Orthographic awareness

A growing body of research evidence counters Smith's (1973) as-sertion that skilful readers do not process individual letters, and from which he deduced that beginning readers do not need this ability. Concerning the differing skills of beginning and experienced readers, the work of Rayner and Pollatsek (1987) lead Adams (1991, p. 23) to write: 'In short, then, skillful readers automatically and quite thoroughly process the component letters of text . . . Ultimately, readers come to look and feel like they recognize words holistically because they have acquired a deep and ready knowledge of the orthographic patterns of their language'. Two large-scale studies (Wells and Raban, 1978; Tizard *et al.*, 1988) highlight the importance of orthographic awareness as a prerequisite for beginning reading and writing, in addition to the possession of concepts about print. These studies reveal that the recognition of and ability to label the letters of the alphabet at school entry is strongly related to reading ability at 7 years of age (with correlations of 0.69 and 0.61, respectively).

Riley's (1994; 1995a, 1996) study provides further evidence of the value of the young reader's refined orthographic knowledge. This is indicated by the ability both to identify and label letters of the alphabet, and by the child being able to write his or her own name before formal school instruction. Riley's findings show that it was possible to predict with 80% accuracy from children's literacy-related entry skills those children who would be reading a few months later at the end of their first year of school.

Phonological awareness

Another crucial factor in the processing of words is phonological awareness, as shown in Figure 2.3. Letters and groups of letters are the constituents of words, representing the sounds of speech. Words are only symbolic representations of units of spoken language; hence the importance of linguistic meaningfulness (Smith, 1971; Goodman, 1973). Unravelling the inter-relatedness of the processing aspects is complicated by the beginning reader's necessity to be able to identify the constituent sounds in words. The ability to distinguish the phonemic segments into which words are divided allows the child to map sound units on to letters and letter groups. In other words, this ability allows access to the alphabetic code system.

After her extensive trawl through the research literature, Adams (1991, p. 42) writes: 'Young readers *must* develop a basic appreciation of the alphabetic system; they must develop a deep and ready knowledge of spellings and spelling-sound correspondences; the capacity to read with fluency and reflective comprehension depends upon it'. The evidence regarding the extent to which the beginner reader and writer is able to hear the sounds in words and link these with his or her reading development gives the teacher of reception and Key Stage 1 pupils valuable clues. Bradley and Bryant (1983) found a causal connection between the ability to detect rhyme and alliterative patterns at preschool and subsequent success in reading at 8 or 9 years of age. A longitudinal study provided further affirmation of the relationship between early rhyming skills and eventual progress with literacy (Bryant *et al.*, 1989). At the beginning stages of conventional reading the young child finds breaking words into their component parts (segmentation) very difficult – and this is an essential skill.

However, Goswami and Bryant (1990) point out that if phonemic analysis is problematic for 5- and 6-year-olds, 'onset' and 'rime' of one-syllable words (i.e. the initial consonant or consonant cluster is the 'onset' and the rest of the word is the 'rime', e.g. *b*-eam and *str*-eam) are not only more comprehensible but are also important speech units for the young child to recognise. An awareness of 'rime' is related to rhyme, and Goswami and Bryant emphasise the value of capitalising on children's natural enjoyment of songs and rhythm. (See also Chapter 1 for further discussion of phonological awareness.)

Implications for practice

Working with the individual child in a supportive and diagnostic way

Nursery and reception classteachers need to be aware of the literacy development of their young pupils. It has already been established that concepts about print are acquired slowly through the emergent literacy phase; they develop through rich and meaningful encounters with print in the twin processes of early reading and primitive message writing. These crucial understandings are the prerequisite to the acquisition of conventional literacy. An integral aspect of this understanding is the growth of the child's gradual appreciation of the symbolic nature as distinct from the formal understanding of written language (Bialystok, 1991) of which the ability to identify and label non-sequential letters of the alphabet at school entry is an early indication. This is very different from the ability to merely recite the alphabet.

Teachers working with young children need to be skilled, diagnostic facilitators of their early literacy attempts. At best they mimic the parent or carer who before school so powerfully assisted valuable literacy progress. At worst, nursery and reception classteachers cut across the child's rich but highly idiosyncratic prior learning to confuse and dishearten (Baker and Raban, 1991).

Clay (1985) has long proposed careful, recorded observations of overt behaviours in the very early stages of beginning reading in order to inform the next step in teaching: 'Sensitive and systematic observation of behaviour is really the only way to monitor gradual shifts across imperfect responding' (Clay, 1991, p. 233). She goes on to list signs of developing inner control in the areas of

- using language (both spoken and 'mark making' written language);
- gaining concepts about print;
- attending to visual information; and
- hearing sounds in sequence.

The beginning reader gradually learns how to integrate the processes, and the teacher needs to monitor the progress analytically. Clay's diagram (see Figure 2.4) shows the four strategies used by the child, and the teacher needs to assess which are the most developed. Teaching follows the monitoring. The first assessment occurs on entry to school. All aspects of the child's processing abilities need to be supported by sharply focused teaching appropriate for the child's developmental stage and level of competence. Effective literacy teaching takes place in a rich, stimulating and well organised learning environment.

A classroom with these qualities has displayed within it evidence of many and various activities that have been shared by the pupils. Literacy acquisition is promoted by giving children satisfying, rewarding and meaningful experiences with print that are integral

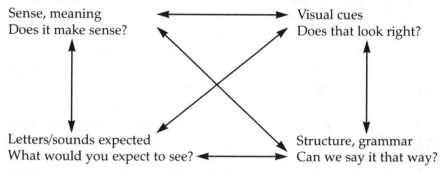

Figure 2.4 Sources of information about text (Clay, 1985)
(From Moll, 1990, p. 207)

both to the ongoing work of the class and to structured teaching linked to the literacy programme. High-quality books and materials to arouse interest, to create intrigue, to promote curiosity and to invite challenge are fundamental to any teaching method.

National Curriculum (pre-level 1)

Observing literacy development

The following list covers some of the behaviours, skills and under-standings that are characteristically displayed by the child at this stage of literacy development:

- *Literacy behaviour* displayed by the child
  - enjoying books;
  - attempting to read known text (acting like a reader); and
  - concentrating on the literacy activity in hand.
- *Understanding* the literacy task is demonstrated by
  - knowing that print has a communicative function;
  - being aware of environmental print, i.e. recognises labels/ notices/messages; and
  - knowing the conventions of print, i.e. can point to where you start reading/knows sweep back on line/knows where to go to on the following page.

Teaching approaches

Children at this stage are in the 'emergent literacy' phase of develo-
ment. They will be able to recognise a few highly distinctive, person-
ally salient words 'logographically'. At this stage of literacy
development the *purpose of print and its conventions* need to be
constantly reinforced. Children, in groups or individually, can be
reminded of how books function during every book-sharing activity.
The teacher should clearly demonstrate

- the print moves from front to back/where the text starts;
- the sweep back on line; and
- the sequence of familiar stories from pictures.

The use of homemade or commercial Big Books and True Image
projectors are invaluable for this.

Prediction skills, using context and syntax, can be encouraged by

- learning stories and poems by heart, especially the use of the class
  poem written on a large sheet of paper;
- telling stories from pictures using picture books with no text;
- retelling stories from memory;
- using picture cues to search for meaning; and
- reading an unfamiliar story, stopping at an appropriate place and
  asking the children to say (or draw) what they think will happen
  next/compare responses.

Phonological development can be encouraged by

- listening to sounds in oral language (bilingual learners should be
  encouraged to do this both in their home language and English) to
  develop phonemic awareness;
- listening to and reciting poems, rhymes, jingles, songs and nursery
  rhymes;
- the explicit teaching of rhyme by learning the written (class) rhyme
  of the week (particularily useful for this are the Dr Seuss titles and
  This is the Bear (Hayes)); by working from books with rhyming text
  (e.g. Jacqui Hawkins' books); and by supplying displays of additional rhyming words;
- introducing letter/sound correspondences through alphabet identification and learning to recognise letters (the use of commercial
  materials, e.g. Letterland, can be helpful here);
- having sufficient copies of high-quality alphabet picture books for
  children to browse through (e.g. Shirley Hughes, Brian Wildsmith);

- placing alphabet friezes round the room (at the appropriate height) and also fixing them with plastic seal to work tables (*Oxford Reading Tree* has produced 'alphabet mats' for use on individual children's work tables);
- using bins of plastic letters (upper and lower case) constantly when undertaking grapheme/phoneme (letter-sound) association work; and
- using games such as deleting first phonemes/'onset', e.g. *b*-us, *J*-ane, *T*-om.

Orthographic development can be encouraged by drawing attention to

- distinctive words in familiar texts, e.g. 'Spot' in *Spot* books;
- familiar words in environmental print, e.g. labels and notices;
- children's names;
- opportunities for mark making and developmental writing both with adults and independently (e.g. making cards, writing letters and notes, labels and notices);
- literacy activities in the home corner, and adaptations of it, e.g. a café, post office, baby clinic, etc.; and
- customised books with familiar repetitive text (photos of the children, their names, familiar logos, e.g. 'Stephen likes *Rice Krispies*' and 'Khadia likes *Weetabix*').

National Curriculum level 1 (early stage)

Observing the child

The following lists of behaviours, skills and understandings are characteristically displayed by children at this stage of literacy development.

Literacy *behaviour* is displayed by

- reading known text with much support;
- pointing word by word as the child or adult reads, i.e. approximate one-to-one correspondence;
- stabbing with a finger at known words, sliding over unknown words; and
- substituting unknown words with no graphic accuracy but with meaning (e.g. house for flat).

Understanding the literacy task is demonstrated by

- being able to discuss books and plot at a literal level; and
- beginning to appreciate that long words when spoken require a correspondingly long symbol when written.

The child's *skills* are demonstrated by

- knowledge of the alphabet;
- beginning to recognise individual high-frequency words out of context;
- being able to point to a letter in a word (this skill often starts with letters in the child's own name);
- being able to read back his or her own caption under a painting; and
- having, towards the *end* of this phase, acquired a small sight vocabulary (possibly 30 words or so) linked to the child's interests/the reading scheme/and high-frequency words around the classroom.

Teaching approaches

Children at this stage are moving from emergent literacy towards conventional beginning reading. They have a sight vocabulary of a few words they recognise 'logographically', and they now need to be supported into the 'alphabetic' phase.

Understanding of the literacy task

Continue to develop *concepts about print* (see suggestions for pre-level 1) and to encourage an awareness that

- print runs from left to right (in English) and from top to bottom, with a sweep back;
- the text can be followed with a finger, demonstrating one-to-one correspondence; and
- it is possible to talk about the author and title of the book.

Predictions skills can be encouraged by the use of context and syntactic cues, and by

- using picture cues to cross-check in the identification of a word;
- anticipating possible sentence structures, e.g. 'Oh, no!' said Mum;
- drawing upon experience to read an unknown word (ensure bilingual children know the English word), i.e. support interrogation of text;

- encouraging the rereading of the sentence to check/confirm meaning and to establish self-correction skills (noting the cueing systems
  available to the child); and
- developing rhyming skills by the use of books with patterned text,
  i.e. ask the child to supply the rhyming couplet (e.g. 'This is the
  bear who fell in the bin/This is the dog who pushed him.')

Phonological development can be supported by

- encouraging recognition of and ability to write each letter of the
  alphabet by emphasising the letter shape, its correct formation *and*
  its sound (always teach letters in handwriting sessions in families,
  e.g. *n h m r*);
- using a flip chart to reinforce the above in whole-class handwriting
  sessions;
- helping awareness of grapheme/phoneme (letter-sound) association through initial sound work, starting with children's names;
- free writing for a range of purposes. The child is encouraged to use
  'developmental writing' or 'invented spelling' in order to represent
  the sounds in words with a symbol. The adult supports with unknown sounds in words, linking them to the alphabet friezes on the
  wall and on tables and to plastic letters. This is a very important
  activity and should be carried out daily. The adult provides feed-
  back (i.e. making things explicit), reinforcing what the child knows
  about the alphabetic system; and
- working in groups on awareness of 'onset' (beginning sound of
  words, consonant or consonant blend e.g. *c*-ab or *cr*-ab) and 'rime'
  (end or following sound, including the vowel e.g. c-*ab* and cr-*ab*)
  both aurally and visually.

Orthographic development (now word recognition) is supported by
helping children to

- make their own books with repetitive texts using photos/names/
  familiar words to represent their ongoing interests;
- recognise their own names from a list of names;
- write their own names correctly, with an emphasis on both letter
  formation and the constituent letters;
- identify and read high-frequency words through writing and games
  located in a meaningful context;
- recognise that length and shape are cues for identifying a word (i.e.
  what the word *looks* like); and

- play games matching word cards to pictures, e.g. photos to children's names, name cards to characters in reading schemes, etc.

National Curriculum level 1 (later stage)

Observing the child

Literacy behaviour is displayed by

- slowing down when reading as the child works hard at processing the text;
- starting to show awareness of mismatch by self-correcting, plus evidence of scanning ahead; and
- spelling becoming more conventional when writing 'developmentally' his or her own text.

Understanding the literacy task is demonstrated by

- being able to use all the four cueing systems – *context* (including picture cue), *syntax* and the *look of the word,* i.e. length/distinctive features, and *phonic analysis* (see Figure 2.4). Strategy use will be erratic, with over-reliance on first one then another cue. Nevertheless, the awareness of the different aspects of print is developing; and
- beginning to consider the plot and character of the story in greater detail.

Skills are demonstrated by an increasing sight vocabulary (approximately 50 words).

Teaching approaches

The activities that are appropriate are the same as for the earlier stages. The child will have moved from the 'logographic' to the 'alphabetic stage' of print processing, and will have both strategies at his or her disposal for reading and writing.

Prediction skills can be developed by using syntax and context, and by

- supporting the use of whichever cue is most appropriate or least automatic, i.e. the weaker strategy for that individual;
- helping in the use of all the cueing strategies (i.e. phonological, orthographic/word recognition and contextual, or context, syn-

tax, look of the word and phonic analysis) over which control is growing (at this stage children need time to use all the cueing strategies);

- helping the prediction of possible sentence structures, especially with books with a highly patterned text;
- talking about characters and motives;
- discussing how the decision was made regarding what the word was;
- praising the child's decoding strategies; and
- making explicit what he or she can do and knows.

Phonological development is supported by

- making explicit the grapheme/phoneme association when reading and writing;
- listening to dominant phonemes (including consonant digraphs *ch*, *sh*);
- blending phonetically regular two- or three-letter words (including nonsense words);
- identifying words that rhyme with familiar sight vocabulary;
- using knowledge of initial sounds to act as a cue when making a choice between two or three words within the sight vocabulary when reading connected text; and
- using analogy to help write new words from known ones, e.g. *shook* from *look*.

Orthographic awareness (print processing/word recognition) is developed by

- practising sight vocabulary with games and context sentence cards (commercial and teacher made), both with and without pictures and whole stories;
- using correct spellings of a few common words in the course of the child's own writing. Attention can be drawn to the standard spelling (of one or two words only) with word lists in the classroom or personal word banks when appropriate and in context.

Additional teaching note

Handwriting practice develops not only the formation of letter shapes but also reinforces grapheme/phoneme association. Also note that it is at this stage that orthographic awareness and phonological awareness become more strongly linked and mutually reinforcing.

National Curriculum level 2

Observing the child

Literacy *behaviour* is displayed by

- being able to read known text independently; and
- beginning to attempt, in a well motivated way, unknown text.

Understanding the literacy task is demonstrated by

- reading more fluently;
- being more able to integrate cueing strategies when decoding an unknown word; and
- being able to discuss stories with insight into character and plot.

Skills are demonstrated by a sight vocabulary of approximately 100 words.

Children will now be moving to the 'orthographic' stage of processing text from the 'alphabetic' stage, i.e. they are able to process groups of letters without letter-by-letter conversion. At times they still use the processing abilities of earlier stages (logographic and alphabetic).

Prediction skills need to be encouraged by the use of contextual and syntactic cues. Self-correction should be supported by cross-checking the four cueing systems when appropriate. This 'scaffolds' (supports) the child and reinforces positive reading behaviours as greater fluency is developed.

Phonological development is supported by helping children to perfect understanding of grapheme/phoneme association in both their reading and writing using 'developmental writing' or 'invented spelling' and

- rhyming words;
- consonant digraphs and blends;
- phonograms (onset and rimes); and
- synthesis of words into syllables.

Orthographic development (word recognition) is supported by

- practising reading sight vocabulary in both text, games and environmental print;
- helping children to spell known words in the course of their own writing by drawing attention to use of word banks, key word lists, etc.;

- encouraging familiarity with letter strings and patterns in words (this can also be done during handwriting practice);
- drawing attention to words with common prefixes and suffixes; and
- helping the decoding of unknown words by analogy with a known word, e.g. *shook/look*.

Additional teaching note

Handwriting is taught concurrently with the above, but not when the child is writing freely and using 'invented spelling' and when composition is the focus.

Organisation of the classroom and literacy activities

Teaching in a structured way within a programme supported by the application of the above suggestions that takes as the starting point the child and her development in literacy and appropriately matches teaching to stage of competence.

But that is not all that the primary teacher has to think about! The wider learning environment is considered in detail in Chapter 5.

3

Supporting Children in Their First Year of School: Four Case Studies

He knew a lot of time: he knew
Gettinguptime, timeyouwereofftime,
Timetogohometime, TVtime,
Timeformykisstime (that was Grantime)
All the important times he knew,
But not half-past two.
                    (Fanthorpe, 1992, pp. 32–3)

The author's research project (Riley, 1994), described earlier, was, by necessity, circumscribed. It was not possible to conduct an in-depth, time-consuming and costly investigation into the observed teaching practices, beliefs and understandings of the reception teachers included in the study. It nevertheless provided invaluable evidence with the finding that it would appear that reception class-teachers hold strongly to a belief that is the *reverse* of the empirical findings on the most important and useful entry skills for literacy progress.

In the questionnaire issued to the teachers, the teachers were asked to rank (in order of importance) the four crucial skills at school entry that are the most predictive of early and successful reading. This was not an easy task. The skills listed (spoken language, concepts about print, the child's ability to write his or her own name and knowledge of the alphabet) are all prerequisites to literacy development. However, the teachers ranked the skills in *reverse* order to the findings in Part 1 of the study. This confirms the value of a well developed print-processing ability at school entry (this is discussed in detail in Chapters 1 and 2).

The crucial issue is that it is important to quantify the levels of progress, given the finding that some classes of children developed faster than others *despite* equable understanding and skills at school entry. But the reason *why* some groups made more progress than others needs to be explored also.

In an attempt to address this issue, data on the differing rates of progress made by four classes were compared to the data from the teachers' questionnaires (an example of the questionnaire can be found in Appendix VI).

The HMI report (1991, p. 6) on *The Teaching and Learning of Reading in Primary Schools* states that 'the contrast between the quality of teaching in the best and worst classes of similar aged pupils in broadly similar circumstances was very stark indeed'. This could also be said of Riley's (1994) findings. The contrasts were surprising, given that the teachers had been chosen by LEA advisers and headteachers on the premise that they were effective. Also, Riley's research was more focused than that of the HMI's, in terms of age phase, geographical location and, of course, size.

Four teachers and their contexts

The children across the whole sample of 191 were assessed at school entry and at the end of the first year of school. This was done to measure the literacy progress they had made (full details of the assessments are given in Appendix II). The new school entrants in the four case study classes had scores in line with the average for the whole group, but by the July of that year, the four classes had made very different rates of progress. Two of the classes had made more progress than might have been expected from the entry skill scores, and two had made rather less than might be expected.

Two more 'effective' teachers: Vera and Annette

These two teachers were very experienced and had spent the majority of their school careers (each over 11 years) teaching reception classes. They both worked with vertically grouped classes, so it was necessary to assess all new September entrants in order to meet the requirements of the project design. Both these teachers taught in a rural county, in schools of approximately just over 200 pupils. They had mixed intakes. Children come from both owner-occupied and council-owned properties. None of the children came from ethnic minorities or were considered to have special educational needs.

The children were admitted to school as 'rising fives' or in the term after they had become 5 years old. This meant that the average age in these classes was slightly higher than the average across the whole sample, and considerably higher than the two comparison classes.

The most interesting feature about these classes is their spread of scores at school entry on those skills considered most predictive of successful reading by the end of the year. Table 3.1 shows the scores of Vera and Annette's pupils compared with the average (mean) score for the whole group of 191 children. Both classes were slightly below average on their understanding of print and its conventions (concepts about print). According to this study, on the two measures that indicate a more refined print awareness, Vera's class was more advanced than the majority of those assessed, but not the most advanced of the 32 classes in the study. Annette's class were more advanced on the measure of the children's ability to write their own names.

Table 3.1   Comparison of mean scores on entry skills between the classes of the more 'effective' teachers and the whole sample ($n = 15$)

	Alphabet knowledge		Ability to write own name		Concepts about print	
	Class	Sample	Class	Sample	Class	Sample
Vera	15.4	9.45	11.5	12.27	6.2	6.35
Annette	7.3	9.45	15.8	12.27	6.1	6.35

These data indicate that the 15 children were functioning well regarding awareness of the task of becoming literate on arrival at school, but not significantly better than the average in the sample. A similar picture emerges for scores on measures that indicate 'general cognitive' functioning.

Two 'less effective' teachers: Janet and Wanda

These two teachers were less experienced than Vera and Annette with the reception age range. Although Janet had been teaching for 11 years in total, only four of them had been spent in reception classes, and Wanda had taught for less than 5 years in total. Both teachers were responsible for small (20 pupil) horizontally grouped classes. Both schools were inner city.

Janet's school had about 150 pupils. Of the intake, 50% were housed on council estates and 50% in owner-occupied homes. The school population comprised 30% ethnic minority pupils and 70% white children. Wanda worked in a school of over 200 children. The vast majority (80%) of the pupils lived in owner-occupied homes, and 10% were described as of ethnic origin. Both these schools (despite their proportions of owner-occupied and council-owned homes so as to fulfil the project criterion for selection – namely, each school population was to have 'a mixed intake') were, nevertheless, operating in less materially advantaged circumstances. The socioeconomic status of the population could be described as working class and upper working class, whereas Vera and Annette's schools drew from a population that could be described as middle and upper working class. The children were chosen from the register by stratified random sampling. That is, the children were selected at random but with a socioeconomic and gender balanced mix.

The children in these classes were young – some of the youngest in the whole sample. The boroughs in which the schools were sited had admissions policies that took pupils the year they became 5 years old. Two of the children were only 4 years and 1 month at the first assessment in September.

Considering their age, a comparison of the entry scores of these two groups with those of Vera and Annette is interesting (see Table 3.2). The spread of the scores on the literacy-related measures was surprising. Janet's children, despite their age, were functioning at the average level and above in their understanding of stories and print, and their ability to discriminate and label letters of the alphabet. However, these very young children were not able to write their names as well as other groups in the sample. Wanda's group were as broadly established in the emergent literacy phase as Annette's group. The children had been exposed to many literacy

Table 3.2 Comparison of mean scores of entry skills between the classes of the less 'effective' teachers and the whole sample (*n* = 17)

	Alphabet knowledge		Ability to write own name		Concepts about print	
	Class	Sample	Class	Sample	Class	Sample
Wanda	10.8	9.45	14.3	12.27	9.0	6.35
Janet	12.0	9.45	8.7	12.70	6.3	6.35

experiences either at home or in their nurseries. From these entry skill scores and those indicating general cognitive functioning, it might be expected that many of these children would be readers by July and were broadly in line with the rest of the sample and the children in Vera and Annette's classes.

Reading progress

Vera and Annette

The children in Vera and Annette's classes had a very successful first year of school. None of the pupils were reading at the beginning of the year but, by July, 13 out of 15 children had achieved a reading age at least in line with their chronological age. One child had a score of 8.9 when 6 years old. Vera's class average (mean) reading age at the end of the year was 6.3, and Annette's was 5.10.

The child who learned most slowly out of the two classes was with Annette. Crispin was not scoring on the Neale's Analysis of Reading test by July. At school entry, Crispin, had a 'draw-a-man' score that indicated he had the representational ability of a child of 3½ years of age, and a similarly low indication of intellectual maturity. His understanding of books and print was very limited, with a score of 2 (out of 12) on the concepts-about-print test. He also knew no letter names or sounds when he arrived at school. However, he made progress in the year. Particularly impressive was his growth in spoken vocabulary, from a score of 88 to 121. He had advanced in all literacy-related measures, and would probably soon be reading well enough to score on a reading test.

The child who scored highest at school entry from the two classes on all measures was in Vera's class, a boy named Adrian. This child was near the ceiling on measures of intellectual maturity. He knew all his letter names and some sounds, and scored the maximum on ability to write his own name. Adrian was clearly well on the road to reading when he arrived in Vera's class and, by the end of the year, he had a reading age of 8. Interestingly, Nathan, a child in Annette's class, came to school with less impressive scores, but was scoring 8.9 on the Neale's Analysis of Reading by July. A close inspection of these data reveals evidence to support the view that Vera and Annette were effective teachers of literacy (full details of the pupils' scores in the four classes are in Appendix VIII).

Wanda and Janet

Wanda was the only teacher in these four case studies who had two children in her class who could read at the beginning of the year. By the end of the year these two pupils had made some progress (one had made only one month's progress on the reading test over the ten-month period). In addition, two other children were scoring 6.7 on the reading test. The other four children had made little progress. Ben came to school scoring 7 (out of 12) on the concepts-about-print test; at the end of the year this had increased to 9. He knew three letter names in September and had learned six more by July. James came to school in possession of all 12 concepts about print, but he could not recognise a single letter of the alphabet; by the end of the year he knew only three letters. The mean scores on the British Picture Vocabulary Test indicated that very low gains had also been achieved in spoken language in this group.

Janet had no children who could read in September, but by July two of her pupils had reading ages of 6.11 and 7. Progress in reading-related measures was evident in the remaining children in the study, but it was not extensive. For example, Lewis came to school with a score of 7 on the concepts-about-print test and, during the year, he gained only one more, and learned seven letter names. In September Natalie knew all her letters and possessed eight concepts about print. However, she had gained no greater understanding of the way books and print work by the end of the year and, needless to say, she was not reading well enough to score on the Neale's Analysis of Reading test.

One of the main findings of the study was that those pupils who did not settle into school easily and well were four times less likely to be reading by the end of the year regardless of the level of their entry skills (this will be expanded in Chapter 4). It might be argued that a possible explanation for the relatively lower levels of progress observed in Wanda and Janet's classes was emotional disturbance owing to poor adjustment to school. However, the average (mean) 'settled into school' scores (as measured on Thompson's *Settled into School* questionnaire, see Appendix V) for the four groups were as follows:

Vera = 38.3
Annette = 45.5
Janet = 38.4
Wanda = 46.1

The classes taught by Vera and Janet settled less well than the other two groups, but the levels of adjustment were approximately equable across the more 'effective' and 'less effective' classes.

Possible explanations for different performances

It has to be acknowledged that the schools of the more 'effective' and 'less effective' teachers were operating in different contexts. Whilst the selection criteria of the research project were fulfilled by using mixed populations in each school, these criteria mean one thing in a shire-county village and something rather different in an inner-city area. As HMI (1991, p. 1) write: 'schools serving areas of marked social and economic disadvantage generally faced much greater difficulties in securing progress in reading than those elsewhere'. They continue: 'The location of the schools was strongly associated with pupils' levels of reading achievement' (*ibid.*, p. 11).

Wanda and Janet were teaching in areas of less material advantage. In their schools were children for whom English was not their first language. There might also have been a higher proportion of children with special educational needs. No pupils with special educational needs were represented in the study, and only one who could be described as coming from an ethnic minority group. However, a comparison between the end-of-nursery scores of the inner-city children in the *Infant School Study* (Tizard *et al.*, 1988) is useful (see Table 3.3). The mean scores of these two inner-city classes indicated that the children in Riley's (1994) study were

Table 3.3 Comparison of the entry skills of two inner-city classes in Riley (1994) and the *Infant School Study* (Tizard *et al.*, 1988)

		Riley (1994): author's version of the test	*Infant School Study* (Tizard *et al.*, 1988): TCRU version of the test
Concepts about print	Wanda's class Janet's class	Mean: 9.0 Mean: 6.3 (possible range 0–12)	Mean: 2.5 (possible range 0–10)
Letter identification	Wanda's class Janet's class	Mean: 10.8 Mean: 11.9 (possible range 0–26)	Mean: 2.4 (possible range 0–26)

Note: TCRU = Thomas Coram Research Unit

considerably more advanced in literacy-related skills and understanding before school than the pupils in the *Infant School Study*
(Tizard *et al.*, 1988).

The children

Janet and Wanda taught the youngest children in the whole of the
study. One of Annette's pupils was the same age at school entry as
the average age of Janet's class in July. This, logically, would
appear to have affected the receptiveness of the two 'less effective'
case-study groups. However, age did not appear to have affected
the children's literacy development or their conceptual maturity as
estimated by their scores on the assessment measures at school
entry. In addition, age was not a statistically significant factor in
the analyses across the sample as a whole.

The *nature* of the children's understanding of the alphabet has
also to be considered. It will be remembered from Chapter 1 that
Bialystok's work (1991) shows that the predictive power of the
children's knowledge of the alphabet stems from their sophisticated and hard-won understanding of the symbolic nature of print.
Those children who had had a prolonged and meaningful exposure to written communication and stories and who were able to
recognise and label letters of the alphabet were further along the
road to beginning conventional reading. The question is, however:
were the pupils in Janet and Wanda's groups functioning at a
symbolic level of true understanding or had they merely been well
taught their alphabet, mechanically and by rote, in their nursery
schools?

A possible answer to this question lies in the acquisition of concepts about print. As has already been argued, a true understanding of the symbolic nature of the letters of the alphabet can only
arise from the prior, and demonstrable, possession of concepts
about print. That is, children could not only identify and label
letters of the alphabet but also had an understanding of the purpose and conventions of print.

As can be seen from Tables 3.1 and 3.2, the pupils in Janet and
Wanda's groups were as advanced on the concepts-about-print
test as those of Vera and Annette. In fact, Wanda's children had the
highest score of the four classes. All the case-study children were
broadly similar across all the literacy and cognitive ability
measures.

Organising the children

The children in the 'less effective' teachers' classes were grouped horizontally; that is, the class contained pupils of the same chronological age. The two 'more effective' teachers operated in vertically grouped classes; that is, not only reception pupils but also Year 1 and Year 2 children. This is especially interesting, given the current debate about the effect of class size on pupil progress.

Based on the finding (Word *et al.*, 1990) that the youngest children benefit from the smallest class sizes, it could be argued that the younger the child, the closer the task must be matched to the pupil (see Chapter 1). In the early years of school in particular, the teacher has to be aware of the child's developmental stage in order to facilitate further progress. In a vertically grouped class, teachers have the opportunity to organise the pupils in such a way that they are able to work with individuals and small groups most effectively. This method of grouping may well have benefited the children in Vera and Annette's classes.

The teachers

Unsurprisingly, the two more successful teachers were the more experienced, both in primary teaching and particularily with this age group. The teaching of the early stages of reading is a highly complex, skilled activity; working with young learners new to a bewildering organisation such as a school demands the most experienced of staff.

Several research projects have shown that the way teachers recount their methods and approaches demonstrates a 'rhetoric/ reality' gap (Mortimore *et al.*, 1988; Tizard *et al.*, 1988). However, the questionnaire that formed a central part of Riley's (1994) research methodology was designed to probe not only what reception class teachers did with their classes but also what they understood of the complex processes involved in the acquisition of literacy. A HMI report (1991) suggests that in 57% of schools the standards for the teaching and learning of reading were high:

> In these schools the teaching of reading was well planned and what was planned was thoroughly implemented resulting in a high level of challenging reading for all children throughout the school.
>
> (HMI, 1991, p. 3)

Poor standards in the remaining 20% as in the previous HMI survey, were strongly associated with weakness in the quality of teaching and in the organisation and management of work in the classroom.

(*ibid.*, p. 2)

In a sense it is a statement of the obvious that the quality of learning depends on the quality of teaching, which needs to be well planned and implemented. Perhaps this *does* need to be acknowledged, given the many approaches involved in teaching the early stages of literacy and the nature of the young child's task in getting to grips with written language. Certainly, the efficacy in the way reception teachers plan, structure and implement high-quality learning experiences for very new school entrants will depend on their level of knowledge of the literacy process and the stages of development of the individuals within their classes.

Vera and Annette demonstrated their substantial knowledge in their replies to the questionnaire. They had acquired this knowledge not only from studying the theory but also by developing their teaching methods in a dynamic and interactive way in line with their understanding. (Vera was especially impressive in the way she operationalised her knowledge.) Both teachers believed that the enjoyment of stories, rhymes and books is the most powerful motivator in learning to read. This is central to any method of teaching reading. Vera and Annette's views overlapped on other prerequisites of beginning conventional reading. They said that children need to have acquired

- concepts about print;
- phonic awareness and word building (indicated by the ability to segment words phonemically);
- an ability to sequence a story; and
- an ability to concentrate.

Regarding the criteria they used to assess the child's stage of literacy development, Vera identified clear, observable behaviours that indicate development as the child moves from emergent literacy to conventional reading. Vera's assessment tools were as follows:

- 'Interest in choosing books to look at and enjoy' (motivation, concentration, enjoyment).
- 'Interest in seeing own stories written and in reading them back' (ability to remember encoding).
- 'Concentration span'.

- 'Ability to match pictures, picture to word, word to word' (indicating an understanding of the symbolic aspect of written language – black squiggles stand for a word, which is immutable. This leads on to more refined understanding that a word is composed of constituent sounds and can be represented graphically).
- ' "Pretend" reading using finger to word' (acting like a reader understanding that speech is continuous, that written language is divided into words, and words into phonemic segments).

Both teachers suggest that they promote early literacy through a range of activities. They encourage storying and sequencing, along with the teaching of phonic awareness and visual discrimination. All the activities centre around meaningful, interesting encounters with print and stories.

This wide-ranging approach is applauded by HMI (1991, p. 7) who assert:

> As in the previous survey, a policy of using a mix of teaching methods was evident in nearly all schools. Teachers rarely adhered to a single method but where they did it invariably failed to meet the needs of a large majority of the children in the class . . . Some of the most successful work established a 'sight' vocabulary. Even those who came to school with a limited grasp of language were taught to recognise familiar words such as their own names and those of common place objects as well as vocabulary associated with the early books of reading schemes. The sound patterns of words were frequently taught so that the children quickly came to see there was usually a correspondence between sounds and letters, or groups of letters. At the same time they were taught to recognise more whole words and short sentences which enabled them to predict patterns of words and to begin to read for meaning. The most effective work made close links from the earliest stages between reading and writing which drew upon the children's familiar experiences at home and school. Successful teachers underpinned these early inroads into reading by engaging children in story reading using good quality books to enrich their understanding of language and fire their interest.

Vera and Annette's classrooms demonstrated all these aspects of good practice, and it is these principles that underpin the suggestions for teaching literacy in Chapter 2. What distinguished these two teachers from the 'less effective' teachers was the recognition of the relationship between teaching and assessment. Annette writes: 'I try to foster a reading community within the classroom.

From that broad base I try to tailor my teaching aims for each child. I plan to take them from the stage I feel that they have reached, to the stage I want them to achieve next.'

Vera was much more detailed in her descriptions of her approaches to teaching various reading strategies at each particular stage of literacy development. Whilst it could be argued that there might be a 'rhetoric/reality gap' and that these teachers did not actually do what they claim they do, the reality is that the children in their classes (according to the data) made the greatest amount of progress of all the 32 classes in the research project.

The research findings cited in Chapters 1 and 2 indicate the need to be *even* more precise and structured than the very best of the teachers in the project described here.

The value of monitoring progress and its link with teaching

Clay (1985) has long promoted close analysis of 'delayed' readers' strategies in order to remedy effectively their confusions and faulty reading behaviours. Regarding all readers, Clay (1991) states that in the first year of school the reception teacher needs to

- analyse from overt reading behaviours the new school entrant's skills and understanding; and
- encourage and develop a range of decoding strategies so that the child extracts meaning from text.

According to Clay's theory of literacy instruction (1972; 1985), all readers, both skilled and inexperienced, have to monitor and integrate information from many sources. Readers need to use, and cross-check, four types of cues:

- Semantic (text meaning).
- Syntactic (sentence structure).
- Visual (graphemes, orthography, format and layout).
- Phonological (the sounds of oral language) (see Figure 2.4, p. 30).

After a year of instruction, 'high progress' readers in New Zealand classrooms, writes Clay (1991), are able to operate and integrate all these sources of cues. They have arrived at the point of achieving a self-improving system. They improve every time they read. As cue users, writes Clay, these children are able to read with their attention focused on meaning, checking several sources of

cues. If higher-level strategies fail, they can engage a lower processing ability to focus on one or another cue source in isolation,
such as letter clusters. However, they also maintain direct attention
on text message at all times.

Low-progress readers, on the other hand, operate with a more
limited range of strategies. Some children rely too heavily on memory, without paying attention to visual details. Others guess words
from the first, initial sound, with little regard for meaning (Clay
and Cazden, 1990).

The Reading Recovery teacher's role, when operating in the one-
to-one remedial teaching programme designed by Clay (1972), is to
analyse closely the strategies the child is using, to make explicit to
the child what he or she is doing and to support the child's active
interaction with the text:

> the teacher creates a lesson format, a scaffold, within which she
> promotes emerging skill, allows the child to work with the familiar,
> introduces the unfamiliar in a measured way, and deals con-
> structively with slips and errors. The teacher calls for the com-
> prehension of texts and for detection and repair of mismatches
> when they occur. She passes more and more control to the child and
> pushes the child, gently but consistently, into independent, con-
> structive activity.
>
> (Clay and Cazden, 1990, p. 209)

Matching the teaching of reading to the individual learner

There is a move towards using this very precise and diagnostic way
of working with *all* early readers, not just with those who are slip-
ping behind. In explaining reading failure, Cashdan (1992, p. 233)
states that 'the selection of methods are not sufficiently diagnostic –
in other words, methods are not precisely fitted to the particular
child and hence there are too many failures who end up needing
special help'. Closely matching the teaching to the child, working
one to one, appears to be crucial in the early stages of transition
between emergent literacy and conventional beginning reading. Although this is difficult in a busy classroom, a skilled teacher can
observe reading and match his or her teaching to these observations
effectively with groups of children. Baker and Raban (1991) write of
the reverse of this principle. They studied a child whose progress
was monitored before school and through the first few months of
school. Baker and Raban used literacy measures devised by Ferreiro
and Teberosky (1982). The 11 tasks were as follows:

1. The formal characteristics a text must possess for reading to occur.
2. The relationship between the text and pictures.
3. Distinguishing between letters and numbers.
4. Distinguishing between letters and punctuation marks.
5. The spatial orientation of text.
6. The relationship between words and pictures.
7. The identification of words in sentences.
8. Do words have to be separate from each other?
9. The effect of transforming words in sentences.
10. What constitutes a reading act?
11. The appropriateness of text to context.
   (Baker and Raban, 1991, p. 8, from Ferreiro and Teberosky, 1982)

After a term in school the little girl had demonstrably regressed, which Baker and Raban sadly attribute to the *inappropriate teaching* she had received. This had taken no account of her prior knowledge and understandings. The most worrying aspect of her deterioration, as Baker and Raban perceived it, was her altered view of herself as a reader and writer. It is hard to imagine that this child's experience was unique. It is Clay's notion of the teacher who first diagnoses the child's literacy stage and then supports progress with direct and sensitive teaching that is further developed in this chapter.

Implications for practice

The role of the teacher

It is necessary to encourage the child to use the most helpful reading strategies (Goodman, 1972; 1973; 1976) to promote positive reading behaviours. The most crucial strategies to develop are the abilities to

- *sample* – the novice reader needs to sample effectively only those details of meaning and print which inform (*or* confirm *or* correct) a prediction about a word. To sample the child needs to use sight vocabulary and salient features about print;
- *predict* – the child learns to predict text based on expectations formed by experience. The reader brings a knowledge of semantic, syntactic and grapho-phonic (letter-sound) expectations to the text (see Figure 2.4. p. 30). These become more refined as the child progresses. Context and picture cues are an important aid,

but the analysis of letters/sounds and the shape and look of words become an increasingly valuable strategy for reducing uncertainty; and

- *confirm* and *self-correct* – the child needs to confirm constantly the accuracy of the predictions and, if inaccurate, to self-correct. As this ability becomes established, the information needed is reduced. Cues are rapidly selected and cross-checked, rereading may occur and certainty confirmed.

Ways to support the development of positive reading strategies

Every time the child reads, the teacher needs to monitor the strategies used sensitively and informally, and to develop overtly the beginning reader's ability to sample, predict, confirm and self-correct. This can be done by drawing attention to appropriate cues, first building on what the pupil already knows of spoken language.

The aim is to encourage independence by praising the child. Useful strategies include such statements as 'Well done! You thought that out! You knew that word from yesterday/the word rhymes with—/you knew it started with *cl* not *cr*'. Observing what the child is *actually doing* when reading indicates what the child knows and understands. This informs what needs to be learned next and therefore taught.

Teaching to support effective sampling

Building a sight vocabulary enables the child to have a bank of rapidly recognised words for use in both reading and writing. This encourages orthographic development which, in turn, facilitates speedy print processing and automatic recognition of patterns and letter groupings and the sounds they represent. The following activities are fundamental and integral to all literacy teaching in the early-years classroom:

- Extensive reading of high-quality texts of many different kinds.
- Frequent transfer of spoken language into written language in meaningful and interesting activities and situations.
- Children writing for themselves and others using familiar words and phrases and using developmental writing (or 'invented spelling').

- Beginning readers need to see and be encouraged to focus upon familiar words and phrases in different and varied contexts, e.g. notices/books/cards/letters in writing for them and by them.

More detailed approaches to support literacy development through the focused teaching of the constituent skills are to be found in Chapter 2.

Teaching to support effective prediction skills

The child needs to be encouraged to make use of both syntactic and semantic cues in order to predict accurately. Teachers can encourage this ability by choosing material of the appropriate level of difficulty. This includes consideration of whether the concepts and vocabulary in the text are within the child's experience. The important point here is that teachers need be knowledgeable about the books they use to capitalise fully on the books' potential learning opportunities. The book should be introduced to the child before it is shared – a technique that is discussed in more detail in Chapter 5.

Teachers can expose the reader to the ideas and words used in the book in preparation for the task of tackling the text. A 'shared' or 'guided' first reading builds on the expectations the child has of the story, of the language structures and the child's knowledge of syntax, e.g. whether the word will be a verb or whether a noun will be singular or plural from the determiners, such as subject/verb agreement.

Cloze procedures or word deletion (both oral and written) are useful in developing this aspect of reading ability – for example, questions such as 'What sort of word would make sense there?' Teachers can encourage the development of orthographic awareness to predict words with questions such as 'What words begin with this group of letters?' This can be followed up with replies such as 'Yes, well done, would that work here?' This is an example of the use of the letter-sound (grapho-phonic) cues available – the 'What makes sense *and* looks right?' strategy.

Teaching to support confirmation and self-correction skills

Once a prediction is made, the reader seeks confirmation. Increasingly minimal information is selected from the cues available and cross-checked. If uncertainty remains, self-correction is needed,

and additional cues are required for consideration. For example, having failed to solve the problem by looking at the initial letter/sound
alone, the child may look at the end of the word. Meaning is called
upon when the child rereads the sentence to check its sense (cross-
checking).

Teachers can support the use of these strategies by making sure of
the following:

- The concepts and language of the text are at an appropriate level of
  difficulty to ensure that cross-checking does not occur so frequently that the meaning is lost.
- The responsibility for confirming the predictions is given to the
  child. Questions such as 'How did you know that was the right
  word?' (sometimes at the end of the piece so that fluency and
  motivation are not sacrificed) and 'Does that make sense?' prompt
  and stimulate positive reading strategies.
- The child is encouraged to use his or her knowledge of the cues
  available. This teaches the child to make decisions about which
  cues are the most useful on different occasions, and hence meaning is reconstructed speedily.

As the child becomes more proficient, the cueing strategies are integrated gradually so that the child achieves what Clay describes as 'the
construction of inner control' (Clay, 1991). Successful readers are
able to make instantaneous decisions – sampling salient features of
text, predicting and then confirming the prediction, all by appropriate
and economical cross-checking.

Clay (1979, p. 6) writes: 'I define reading as a message-gaining,
problem-solving activity, which increases in power and flexibility the
more it is practised.' Once the child can *integrate* all four cueing
strategies, he or she will improve every time he or she reads.

Teaching to support the child's integration of strategies

A child with few decoding strategies at his or her disposal will rely
too heavily on a narrow repertoire, and will permanently struggle to
make sense of text – except very familiar, well-known and favourite
books. The skilled monitoring of the child's reading through observation will help the teacher to identify precisely what the reader can
do, and which strategies need developing.

As the teacher is observing the child working on text, it is important
that

- the teacher does not intervene too early;
- the child is encouraged to show independent problem-solving strategies;
- meaning and sense are the prime cues for confirming and cross-checking;
- rereading pulls together the available information to make the sentence (or phrase) whole and to clarify meaning; and
- the child is directed to lower-level strategies of grapheme-phoneme (letter-sound) correspondence and the shape or 'look' of the word.

These principles underpin all literacy teaching, with both individuals and groups.

Observation of the child's growing grapheme-phoneme (letter-sound) awareness demonstrated through writing

In reading, the goal is access to meaning. This is achieved through the strategies of whole-word shape, context and decoding by grapheme-phoneme and orthographic processing. Writing is often letter-by-letter grapho-motor production. Both processes contribute to literacy acquisition, as they develop side by side and are complementary to each other.

The importance of writing in the young child's literacy development is confirmed by much research evidence (Clay, 1972; Goodman, 1976; Smith, 1978; Bissex, 1980; Ferreiro and Teberosky,
1982). This importance is well described by Ferreiro (1985, p. 84)
when she writes: 'Let us accept that those children, when they write,
make an approximate correspondence between sounds and letters.
They may face orthography problems, but they do not have any
further problems with writing, because they are now functioning in-
side the alphabet system of writing.'

As the child writes, he or she actively struggles with the
orthographic and phonological processors (see Figure 2.1, p. 22). The
child converts the sounds he or she can hear in parts of words into
symbols on the paper. To do this, the child uses 'invented spelling' or
'developmental' writing. This approach provides the teacher with a
valuable opportunity to analyse literacy development. When invent-
ing spellings, the child tends to move through stages of development
which gradually become more refined and conventional (Gentry,
1981). These stages are as follows.

Precommunication

At this stage the young writer indicates that he or she knows that
symbols can represent speech. The writing will be a rough approx-
imation of known letters or numbers. Often the letters of the child's
own name are used repeatedly and in random order.

Semi-phonetic

One-, two- and three-letter spellings show some representation of
letter-sound (grapheme-phoneme) correspondence, e.g. *wnt* = went,
dg = dog, *p* = please.

Phonetic

Now the writer has almost perfect grapheme-phoneme match. The
child develops the ability to segment words phonologically, e.g.
becos = because, *wot* = what, *sed* = said.

Transitional

At this period of literacy development, the child is in the orthographic
stage of reading and is able to process groups of letters without letter-

by-letter conversion. In writing, the child is able to move towards conventional spelling. The ability to process 'chunks' of words enables the 'look' of a word to be remembered. Familiar patterns from a working sight vocabulary can be utilised correctly, e.g. *huose* = house, *eightee* = eighty.

At this stage the child appreciates that in English the same sound can be represented by different groups of letters, e.g. *ay*, *ai* or *a*.

Developmental writing (or 'invented spelling') demonstrates the writer's developing awareness of

- alphabet and letter names;
- letter-sound relationships;
- directional rules;
- concepts of a letter or a word;
- the functions of space;
- the ordering of letters in a word;
- the sequence of sounds within a word; and
- punctuation.

Monitoring literacy development

The potential for the young child's progress to be erratic or unbalanced is immense, given the complexity of the literacy process. And this even before the issue of individual learning styles or particular difficulties is considered. Therefore, monitoring is essential. This is not a new principle to an early-years teacher – the adage *observe*, *support* and *extend* is a fundamental part of the professional repertoire.

The main reasons for regular monitoring are to

- establish what each individual can do;
- identify what strategies the child is using;
- assess individual stage and rate of development;
- enable the teacher to provide appropriately for the individual and/ or small groups;
- inform the choice of appropriate materials; and
- ensure appropriate organisational strategies are used, e.g. different groupings of children.

Monitoring follows the assess/plan/teach/assess cycle of primary teaching, and is integral to the literacy programme. It needs to be carried out at regular intervals. Clay proposes that a written record should be made every three weeks so that reading progress can be carefully checked and supported.

Monitoring should occur at different levels during normal teaching sessions. Classroom organisation can be arranged so that there is opportunity to assess one or two children daily (see Chapter 5). Formal monitoring follows assessment on arrival at school (see Chapter 1). Experienced teachers constantly observe children while they are learning, and this diagnostic observation informs teaching.

More formal monitoring involves assessing and recording the child's development regarding

- essential understandings about print and its conventions;
- the strategies used when reading continuous text; and
- attitudes to literacy.

Specific skills and abilities that need to be assessed are

- how well directionality and one-to-one matching are established;
- the extent to which the child uses the strategies of sampling, predicting, confirming and self-correction;
- the child's appropriate use of available cues;
- the extent to which the child's use of cues is integrated;
- the child's ability to reconstruct the meaning of the text;
- the extent of the child's sight vocabulary;
- the child's ability to hear sounds in words (i.e. to segment phonemically) and to map the sounds on to symbols with an increasing accuracy in the child's appreciation of the vagaries of the English language; and
- the stage of the child's writing development, in particular with invented spellings.

As Holdaway (1979, p. 168) says, 'the best policy is to monitor actual behaviour as the child carries out the task in a meaningful situation – such as normal reading and writing within the programme – and to compare such observations with those taken for the same child at some previous time'.

If a teacher observes one or two children daily using such techniques as 'miscue analysis' or 'running reading record', this will ensure that all the pupils in the class are formally assessed approximately once a month. Such records monitor reading (processing) behaviour as the reader works on an unfamiliar text. Pupils causing concern may need more frequent monitoring. Children progress at different rates and are at different stages of development: teachers need to be aware of this to ensure that class provision constantly matches their changing literacy needs.

Running reading records and miscue analysis

When the child is working on an unfamiliar text, the teacher is able to observe how the child is processing the text. This allows the teacher to assess how the child

- is reconstructing meaning;
- is taking risks;
- is using available cues;
- uses those cues which are most developed;
- chooses the most appropriate cues; and
- integrates strategies.

Both these methods of assessing reading behaviour record the level of accuracy on an unfamiliar text, largely unaided, and in addition, uses the child's errors or 'miscues' as the focus for analysis in determining the processing abilities of the reader as he or she utilises the cues available. (Examples of 'running reading records' are given in Appendix IX.)

4

Positive School Adjustment and Success with Reading

Eleven new children came in on Monday – 2 days ago. The teacher tells me they are awful – lots of tears and crying for Mummy – even at five past nine! It is getting her down. The room seems crowded with tables and chairs.

8.55 a.m. Children start to come in because it is raining. Usually they have to wait in the playground until the bell goes. The teacher is writing on the blackboard for the older ones, she occasionally comments to a child. One new child cries. The teacher is talking to another parent and takes no notice. The parent helper goes to the child and distracts him with drawing.

9.00 a.m. A child goes to the teacher holding up his arms and crying. 'Sit down,' she says, pushing him towards a table. He sits by a helper who reaches for him. Three children are crying now by the parent helper. All need her arms, she tries to touch them all. The teacher shouts at a boy, 'John, that is enough, we'll all cry in a minute.' She tells him off. A boy is dragged into the classroom by the teacher. The teacher and helper go out leaving three crying, one is holding the helper's hand when she comes back.

9.06 a.m. The teacher says sharply 'All line up by the door.' She claps her hands. Two crying children are dragged into the line, one forced to leave his new pencil case on the table. T. 'Stop that, you're a big boy now.'

Assembly. The infant classes are told they will have to undress after play 'to have apparatus.' A child cries. Back to class.

9.45 a.m. Register.

Teacher: 'After play we are doing apparatus.' A child cries. She is told off. No other explanation about P.E.

(Bennett and Kell, 1989, p. 41)

Research evidence suggests that a successful, early start with learning to read is dependent on the child's level of adjustment to school. Factors that determine the child's adjustment to mainstream school include the challenges presented by the school and the individual's personality and temperament. The effect of positive or negative adjustment on the level of overall functioning is now clearer. Newson and Newson (1977, p. 45) write:

> When we say that children adjust or 'settle down' to school then we may be in danger of missing the crucial point: that they are being subjected to a compelling socialisation process much of which offers persuasive rewards, but as a result of which they learn to accept their place as very junior members of an elaborate social hierarchy.

Thus the factors that dictate the child's adaptation to this socialisation and allow sufficient emotional and intellectual energy to support learning are complex.

The challenges of school for the new school entrant

In the early 1980s, several studies focused on the experience of adjustment to school. The difficulties children have in coping with the discontinuity between home and school are documented by Cleave *et al.* (1982). These researchers looked at such factors as the physical environment, the institutional routines and the language used by the adults, as well as the problems they presented to the young entrant. The size of the buildings, the nature of the artificially segmented school day and the ways in which the children were spoken to by adults all presented difficulties for the bewildered young pupils. Willes (1983) focused on the language teachers used in questioning, and found this to be very different from that used by parents and carers at home.

Barratt (1986) found many variables across 76 reception classes when evaluating the experience of starting school. However, the strangeness of the situation was greatly alleviated by the personal warmth and skill of experienced reception teachers. Much seemed to depend on the extent to which the teacher was able to empathise with the child. This crucial ability to ease the trauma of separation from parents or carers for long periods of time involved having appropriate expectations in the early days and beyond, which had a positive effect on the way the child settled.

In the study undertaken by Riley (1994), reception class teachers responded to a postal questionnaire (see Appendix VI). In response to a question concerning their declared aims for the first year of school, the teachers stated that they viewed social considerations as marginally more important than academic aims – at least initially. This indicates an understanding of the child's need to be emotionally secure in order to learn successfully, and an implicit regard of the whole child and his or her developmental needs, which typify teachers of the early years.

It was suggested in Chapter 3 that, unsurprisingly, the most effective reception class teachers investigated in the project were those with the most experience of the reception-year age group. This implies also that they were skilled at tuning in to the emotional and psychological needs of the new school entrant as well as to their stage of literacy, on arrival at school. This is an important consideration for headteachers to address when allocating teachers to classes. Given the accumulating evidence about the importance of the first year of school, it would seem logical that the most competent, experienced and empathetic teachers should be allocated to the reception class.

Predisposing factors within the child

An individual's ability to withstand stress depends both on his or her temperament and his or her ability to learn coping mechanisms. The transition to school draws hugely upon the young pupil's inner resources regarding emotional stability and the ability to be flexibile. Other factors, such as introvert or extrovert tendencies as well as the child's preschool experience, will influence the coping strategies. Those children without siblings frequently find school and its demands (the need to share adults, equipment and toys) more difficult than those from larger families who are used to interacting with brothers and sisters.

Clearly, the extent to which the school entrant is prepared for the days following admission has a great deal to do with the extent the child is able to adjust. Preparedness for school was studied by Chazan *et al.* (1971). Children were assessed on an interview, which rated them as poorly prepared or well prepared for school. Factors from the child's previous experience thought to be relevant to starting school were considered: familiarity with books, nursery rhymes, the scale of provision of play materials at home and opportunities to meet the other children before school entry. This reflects the importance of the child 'knowing what to do' (Barratt, 1986). The conclusion of Chazan *et al.* (1971) was that the degree to which a child was well prepared for school relates to socioeconomic aspects of the parents' backgrounds, such as their attitudes to education. Much research could still be carried out in this area.

School adjustment and a successful start to learning

The link between adjustment and learning is less well documented. Clark (1976) found that those children who read easily and early tend to be those who settle into school happily. Conversely, Hughes *et al.* (1979) have shown that some children do not find school a conducive environment for learning.

Earlier studies (Ilg and Ames, 1965; Johannsen, 1965; Austin and Lafferty, 1968) suggested a positive relationship between school readiness and later educational performance. The child who is ready for school, and hence makes a satisfactory adjustment to it, is more likely to be successful in the rest of his or her educational career than the child who is not ready. Thompson developed a scale that focused on three areas of behaviour that might be indicative of how well a child is coping with school:

1) *Emotional adjustment*   This focused on the child's independence and self-reliance and the extent to which the child could accept criticism and admonishment.
2) *Social adjustment*   This area of functioning explored whether the child is able to relate satisfactorily to adults and peers.
3) *Attitude and behaviour in response to intellectual demands*   This area investigated the extent to which the child is interested in his or her work, concentrates, involves him or herself and uses time and opportunities valuably.

In Thompson's study (1975) a 24-point scale questionnaire was completed for 137 children after they had been in school half a term. The samples were divided into two. In one half of the sample, the results demonstrated that those children who had attended nursery school were rated more favourably by their teachers in the cognitive area of functioning than children who had not attended preschool. In the other half, attendance at nursery school was not positively related to settling into school and coping well with the school's demands.

By following the progress of two cohorts of children through their first year of school, Riley (1994) was able to quantify the effect of a positive adjustment to school. In addition to assessing the children, the class teachers were asked to complete the Thompson *Settled into*

School questionnaire on each child after he or she had been at school for a period of six weeks. The main findings are as follows.

A wider range of functioning was shown (see Appendix VII) across the sample at school entry than the mere 15-month spread of chronological age might indicate. At the lowest end of the concepts-about-print test, some children had a score of 3. This means that they understand so little about books and their conventions that they know only the direction of the book and the print and that the text not the pictures tells the story. Some children knew no letters of the alphabet; on the other hand, one child had a reading age of 8.3 on the Neale's Analysis of Reading test.

However, the most interesting findings were from those measures that related positively to reading at the end of one year in school. The analyses showed that certain literacy-related skills were highly indicative of later success with reading. Figure 4.1 shows the strength of the relationship between the reading-related skills and the end-of-year reading score (as measured by the Neale's Analysis of Reading score).

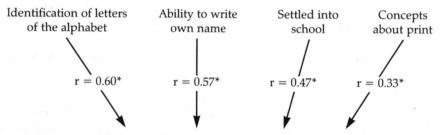

Neale's Analysis of Reading score in July (at end of the year)

Figure 4.1 A summary of the relationship between entry skills and reading at the end of the first year (The 'settled into school' score indicates the third strongest association with later success in reading; $*p < 0.001$)

This assessment (Thompson questionnaire, see Appendix V) was completed by the teacher after the child had been in school six weeks. It proved to be a valuable predictor of later success in literacy. Surprisingly, the extent to which the child had settled into school appeared to be unrelated to how old the child was at school entry (the intercorrelation of entry skills showed a non-significant $r = .004$ correlation between the age of the child and the 'settled into school' score). The significance of this will be discussed later.

The power of the child's positive adjustment to school to predict success in reading was further investigated using a statistical technique called 'forced multiple regression'. This analysis takes account of all factors simultaneously, and quantifies the individual contribution each of the entry skills makes to the Neale's Analysis of Reading score at the end of the year.

By categorising children into groups according to their 'settled into school' score, it was possible to refine this strong association between early school adjustment and reading further (see Table 4.1). Of the 18% of children who were still unsettled after six weeks in school, only seven were reading by July. Of the 33% of children who settled well into school, 48 of the 64 were reading well enough to score on the Neale's Analysis of Reading test in July, whatever their entry skills.

Table 4.1 'Settled into school' scores ($n = 191$)

	Non-readers	Readers
Very settled	16 (8%)	48 (25%)
Settling	45 (23.6%)	47 (24.6%)
Unsettled	28 (14.7%)	7 (3.7%)

According to Riley's (1994) findings, the extent to which a child has adjusted positively to school appears to be an important factor in being able to read by the end of the year. Further statistical analyses (chi-square) were carried out to determine the level of the statistical significance of the relationship between the 'settled into school' score and the ability to read (as measured by the Neale's Analysis of Reading test). (The figures used in this analysis can be found in Appendix IV.)

Implications for practice

The main findings of this study are that those children who enter the reception class with

- a well developed knowledge of the alphabet;
- an ability to write their own names;

- an understanding of the concepts about print; and
- a positive adjustment to school

have an 80% chance of reading (at least in line with their chrono-logical age) by July of the same academic year. It is important that these factors are better understood by teachers and parents as they have important implications for teaching in the reception year.

Of the sample of 191, 54% were reading well enough by the end of the year to score on the Neale's Analysis of Reading test, and others had made progress in reading-related skills. Of these readers, 93% were described as adjusting well to school or were settling. Only 3% of the whole group who had been described by their teachers as unsettled halfway through the autumn term were read-ing by July.

It is not surprising that those children who found school bewilder-ing or unpleasant did not succeed in the task of learning to read. Clark (1976) found that her early readers had settled happily into school. Using the under-reacting scale of the Bristol Social Adjustment Guide, Wells and Raban (1978) found that those children with higher scores were likely to have a lower measured reading attainment at the age of 7. The researchers found that quiet, miserable children were underfunctioning and continued to do so through their second year because of poor school adjustment. These quiet, underfunctioning children were encountered more frequently than children who exhibited behavioural problems – children displaying more overtly 'acting out' behaviour. Other large-scale studies that monitored progress through the early years, such as *The Infant School Study* (Tizard *et al.*, 1988), did not assess adjustment to school.

Across the six LEAs involved in the project (Riley, 1994), admissions policies varied, as did the age at which the children started school. Given the research literature that has emerged regarding the difficulties school presents to 4-year-olds (Cleave and Brown, 1991), it is interesting to note that, in the present study, the child's age at school entry is not associated with how well he or she adjusted to school ($r = .004$). Some of the children were as young as 4.1 at the time of the assessments. Other factors than age proved to be more influential:

- Ability to identify and label letters of the alphabet.
- Ability to write own name.
- The extent to which the child has settled into school.
- Understanding concepts about print.

However, as has been discussed in Chapter 3, it should be recognised that the child's maturity may affect his or her ability to concentrate and to persist at a task.

The findings about the link between adjustment to school and successful learning further complicate the issue of how primary schools provide the most positive environment for learning. It is not surprising that the child needs to feel secure and happy in order to deploy all his or her faculties fully to meet the challenge of acquiring literacy. Reception classteachers need to be aware of this. Only then is it possible to have an informed basis on which to consider admission policies, the reception class environment and organisational structures – in addition to capitalising on the rich but highly idiosyncratic knowledge pupils possess about literacy.

Admission policies

The main theme of this book is that the young child is extraordinarily capable, as Donaldson (1989, p. 36) writes:

> children are highly active and efficient learners, competent enquirers, eager to understand. . . .

> Children's minds are not at any stage – not ever – to be thought of as receptacles into which stuff called knowledge can be poured. Nor do children wait in a general way for us to prod them into learning. They wonder, they question, they try to make sense. And, not infrequently, when they direct their questions at us they push to the limit our ability to answer them, as every adult who has spoken much with children knows.

Donaldson goes on to say that this enormous potential is unique to each individual and is motivated by different interests. The research evidence that begs for each young school entrant to receive due and individualised consideration, has layered upon it that the young pupil needs to feel secure and at ease in order to continue to develop the learning achieved prior to school. The first major factor new pupils encounter in their adjustment to school is the manner in which their first acquaintance with the school is organised.

Links with preschool establishments

Thought and time has to be given to meet the needs of every new pupil and to make the transition from home to school as smooth as possible. One proven way of easing the trauma of entry to school for 4 and 5-year-olds is to make links with the feeder nursery schools and play groups. As the HMCI report (DfE, 1993, p. 2) states: 'About 90% of the children had attended some form of pre-school provision. Most of the schools had links with the main playgroups, nursery classes and nursery schools which the children had attended, but the level and quality of this contact differed considerably.' The report continues (*ibid.*, p. 6): 'Where induction arrangements were poor, it was sometimes because pupils began school full-time too abruptly with little opportunity to visit beforehand or for a short period of part-time attendance . . . when more gradual induction became the norm this was widely accepted as beneficial.' School policies which operationalise this philosophy will organise visits to the preschool setting by the reception class teacher or the nursery nurse, or the child may visit the reception class from the preschool.

Arrangements need to take into account the availability of staff and the numbers that can be accommodated with ease. This will ensure the visits are calm, well organised and relaxed. Visits by school staff to the child's home for particular purposes (such as visiting a child with special needs or who may be at risk in some way) are of great benefit.

A phased start to school

The majority of primary schools now provide a gradual, gentle start for their new intakes. This gives the new children the opportunity to experience a shorter school day and to be members of a smaller group than normal for the first few weeks. Educationally this makes good sense: it provides the teacher with the opportunity to observe closely and form relationships with the new pupils. The contact with parents at the beginning and end of each school day is invaluable for deepening the teacher's understanding of the child as an individual. Cleave and Brown (1994, p. 8) give examples of different patterns of staggered school entry:

- all new entrants admitted over two days;
- a third of the class admitted daily for three days;
- all the class admitted at half-hourly intervals during the morning throughout the week;
- small groups admitted on alternate days;
- no new children admitted until the established (mixed-age) class were settled.

Children admitted before statutory school age provide the school with greater flexibility. Arrangements can be made individually, such as part-time attendance for all those not yet 5 years old or, in the case of those LEAs that admit children the year they become 5, for the first half term. The resulting paced start has been found by HMCI (DfE, 1993) to have positive and long-lasting effects on personal adjustment, and hence on learning.

Staffing

The issue of staffing is one of quality and quantity. The calibre and level of human resourcing is clearly the major factor in the child's success on entry to school. The issue of the level (as it refers to the numbers, type of training and educational background and the extent of early-years experience of the staff) is addressed in the HMCI report (DfE, 1993, p. 10): 'standards were usually better in classes with two adults' and 'non-teaching assistance made an important contribution to standards and quality. This was invariably better where the assistant had suitable qualifications.' This is in line with the findings of the Word *et al.* (1990) project on class size and Riley (1994). To every reception and early-years teacher it would be merely to state the obvious that higher levels in both quality and numbers of staff, results in a more effective learning experience for the child.

Where there is a commitment to working with children in small groups and where individual observations are carried out, Cleave and Brown (1994) found that schools used parents and retired people to help in the classroom. However, voluntary help is not without its problems, and it places additional demands on the teacher.

The use of trained teachers with appropriate expertise and experience has also to be considered. Working with new school entrants requires specialist knowledge at best, and at the very least an early-years training. Too often it is assumed that working with very young children requires little more than a high degree of warmth, patience and other such attributes found in a good mother.

The first step to overcoming this problem is the recognition of the fact that not all primary teachers are well suited to or equipped for this work; the second is to address how the situation can be rectified on a practical level. Again, Cleave and Brown (*ibid.*, p. 13) offer some suggestions:

The teachers in our study increased their expertise by:

- working alongside more experienced colleagues;
- working with advisers and advisory teachers;
- attending courses and conferences and undertaking advanced study in early years education;
- establishing support groups and networks;
- visiting other schools.

Inevitably, this issue is interwoven with class size, which was discussed in Chapter 1. The UK government has refused to acknowledge, let alone act upon, American research findings on the enduring benefit of smaller class sizes, especially for the early years. Smaller class sizes have resource implications, but the benefits to staff further up the school of a successful start to literacy and the rest of the curriculum are obvious, not least in longer-term financial savings.

It would seem that a temporary solution to this lies, at least in part, in the hands of headteachers and governing bodies, given their increased control over personnel and the internal organisation of the school. In the longer term, it must be recognised that a more equable funding formula is necessary, in line at least with that of secondary schools. As Bennett (1996, p. 54) says:

it has to be accepted that to provide smaller classes (across the whole primary school) would be extemely expensive. The best compromise might be, therefore, to begin in a limited way by implementing this process in the reception class. The learning boost that this can provide would not only provide lasting benefits to the children themselves, but would also provide enduring value for money.

Teaching issues concerning class organisation and teaching techniques will be addressed in the next chapter.

5

The Organisation of a Learning Environment

Reading programmes should be child centred.
Reading for meaning is paramount.
Reading must always be rewarding.
Children learn to read by reading.
Children learn best on books that have meaning and are rewarding.
The best approach to teaching reading is a combination of approaches.
The best cure for reading failure is good first teaching.
The foundations of literacy are laid in the early years.

(Statement on the teaching of reading
by the Ministry of Education, New Zealand, 1995)

The first four chapters of this book have drawn attention to issues concerning

- the first year of school;
- the complexity of the literacy process;
- the characteristics of effective literacy teachers in the early years; and
- the link between success with reading and positive adjustment to school.

For the teaching of literacy to be effective, the significance of these factors must be recognised and the nature of their dynamic inter-relationship understood as the basis for a multifaceted approach.

Effective literacy teaching

Children will flourish as readers when

- they are taught by a knowledgeable, empathetic, sensitive and warm teacher;

- a well organised environment provides a carefully chosen range of print and text;
- they experience a balanced structured programme that

  - enables and monitors progression at each individual's level;
  - provides opportunities for each child to gain confidence and satisfaction;
  - maintains interest with meaningful and varied tasks; and
  - offers structured support and teaching at the whole/small-group and individual levels; and

- the classroom organisation

  - enables each child to receive the appropriate amount of attention; and
  - allows space and opportunity for the teacher to encourage, assist, monitor and guide.

General principles of a literacy programme

In common with successful teaching and learning in other areas of the curriculum, the literacy classteacher has to promote a warm, positive and enabling environment that encourages independence and risk taking in all pupils. Clay (1979) has long advocated an active and constructive approach to the teaching of reading and writing. In this way, the young readers are encouraged to rely on their problem-solving abilities in the search for fluency.

As was seen in Chapter 3, the teacher's role is complex. Fisher (1992, p. 7) encapsulates this well when she writes:

A picture emerges of a teacher with an important and specific role to play. Someone who is far more than a didactic figure imparting knowledge, and more again than only a facilitator who expects learning to take place from no more than the provision of a stimulating environment and some good books.

The teacher is someone who can facilitate learning by the range of provision in the classroom; one who can lead a child to understanding of the task by modelling attitudes and behaviour that are crucial to lasting development; one who can manage the learning situation in order to enable children to achieve their potential; and, most importantly, one who can observe and assess children's performance in order to ensure that the other roles work effectively for the individual child.

There are three understandings that underlie all aspects of organisation and teaching in the early-years classroom, they are in connection with:

- books;
- the reading process; and
- written text.

Books

Books are a source of interest and delight, challenge and stimulation. Books provide information, answers to questions and extend our view of the world by revealing new possibilities. The messages children learn from high-quality books are described by Meek (1988) as the 'untaught lessons' of texts:

- How the book works and the structure of stories.
- The way the reader interacts and works with the text (e.g. the fact that the fox is not mentioned anywhere in the text in *Rosie's Walk* (Hutchins, 1968)).
- An appreciation of metaphor, i.e. the meaning of text is more than its face value.
- The nature and variety of discourse.
- Texts are polysemic, using allusion and intertext (e.g. *The Jolly Postman* (Ahlberg and Ahlberg, 1986)).
- The content of the story and the way different value systems are represented in books.

Books of enduring quality are those that withstand multiple readings and those that offer the potential for interpretation at a variety of levels, and can thus be revisited with renewed interest. Such books include those not only written for children as story books but also some of those written for structured reading schemes.

In many schools, teachers use a combination of different types of books to teach reading rather than relying solely on either a structured reading scheme or selected children's literature. The reader's growing competence has to be catered for with books of an appropriate level of complexity of content and difficulty of text.

Whilst the subject-matter is the prime consideration, books that are structured (i.e. published reading schemes) take into account the following factors:

- The content.
- The background experience of the intended audience of pupils.

- The structure and style of the story.
- The complexity of language.
- The vocabulary (some reading schemes have a 'controlled' vocabulary and/or capitalise on repetition).
- The illustrations.
- The size and layout of print.
- The relationship between the text and the illustrations, which includes the amount of text relating to each illustration, thus affecting the reading level.

The following conditions should be borne in mind when selecting books for use with a child or group of children:

- The child's stage of reading development (see Chapter 2).
- The book's level of difficulty.
- The particular teaching opportunities in the book (i.e. the way the illustrations encourage prediction in such books as *The Spooky Old Tree*).
- The approach the teacher will be employing with the child (shared, guided or independent reading; see below).

National Curriculum (pre-level 1)

The books used will enable the emergent reader to

- enjoy literature;
- appreciate the unchanging nature of print;
- learn the conventions of print;
- understand that the illustrations allow prediction of what is going to happen; and
- appreciate the rhythm and repetition of language.

By the end of this stage the child is

- beginning to attempt to read the text unaided;
- able to predict (can make suggestions about what might happen in the story); and
- able to recognise words in a number of contexts.

National Curriculum (early and later level 1)

The books used will enable the beginning conventional reader to

- draw on wider-ranging experiences and understandings;

- extend his or her vocabulary; and
- use more complex and varied language structures.

During this crucial stage of reading development, children need to be encouraged to make meaning from text by

- using their background experience;
- problem-solving through taking risks and making approximations;
- using both text and illustrations to sample, predict and confirm predictions;
- rereading and reading on to gain meaning;
- using grapheme-phoneme association to confirm the prediction of a word;
- self-correcting; and
- beginning to integrate the cueing strategies.

National Curriculum (level 2)

The books used at this level will enable the fluent reader to

- encounter different types and styles of writing;
- experience indirect and direct speech structures;
- read more complex grammar; and
- become familiar with a wide range of adjectives and adverbs.

By the end of this stage the child is confidently and competently able to

- integrate all the cueing systems;
- maintain meaning over complex sentences in both prose and poetry;
- adjust the reading rate for the purpose, i.e. to scan and skim for information; and
- express opinions based upon what has been read, e.g. regarding the style of the book or the characters.

The reading process

Being able to read fluently requires the following:

- Meaning is accessed by integrating the information gained from several cues in the text.
- Appreciating that some cues are more useful than others.

- Risk taking when working on a text.
- The flexible use of the available cues that enable independent, satisfying and efficient reading.

The written text

Written text is a symbolic representation of spoken language. Understanding this principle involves an appreciation that different sounds in words can be separated out (phonemic segmentation) and mapped on to letters and groups of letters in order to construct meaning – both at word and sentence level. It also involves an appreciation that print has its own conventions, which are consistent, and that print almost always makes sense.

It is the main aim of the class teacher to promote active readers. Successful readers share the following characteristics:

- An enjoyment of books and the ability to find in them ideas and stories that enrich the readers' lives.
- The capacity to reconstruct meaning every time they read.
- The confidence to read independently, and consequently to improve every time they read and write.

Readers who develop in this way are those who have been taught in a stimulating and challenging literacy environment. A range of teaching approaches will have been used to foster appropriate *positive attitudes* towards reading. It is the main aim of classteachers to promote *active* reading.

The learning environment

An enabling learning environment for literacy also has to be one that promotes the development of oracy. In the years before school, almost all children have acquired a wide vocabulary and learned how to employ a complex system of grammar. More importantly, the child has learned that each individual is able to make his or her own meaning (Halliday, 1975).

Through spoken language the child is able to structure experience, to make sense and to communicate. In addition, written language increasingly supports intellectual development and extends children's understandings of the world and people. Therefore, the teacher needs to view oracy and literacy as inter-related. The classroom needs to offer rich experience, activity and stimulation that promote the talking from which reading and writing will naturally arise.

It must be remembered that, before school, play has been the vehicle through which much powerful language learning has occurred. Meek (1982, p. 33) says:

> The child talks to his toys about past events and goes over what has happened in different ways of explaining and telling:
>
> 'This is my mummy house, my daddy house,
> my Billy house, my granny house,
> Houses, houses, houses, his houses,
> and mummy goes to work and Billy . . .'
>
> For all that seems inconsequential, this early talk is by no means random. It performs many functions in children's language learning, but its relevance here is that it is story-telling, the beginning of knowing how to narrate.

The teacher needs to harness the pupil's predilection to play, to talk and to make-believe by providing challenging classroom opportunities to engage in such activities. The home corner can be

converted into any current class preoccupation (a hospital, a post-office, McDonald's, a travel agent, a book shop or whatever) to stimulate activity, fantasy, language and literacy.

The benefits of a well organised classroom to a teacher are obvious, but the benefits to literacy learning need to be made explicit while considering the general principles. Language is greatly enhanced by a classroom that has an organisational system that supports children's developing autonomy and the growth of their confidence and self-reliance. Autonomy also provides the teacher with the time and opportunity to observe literacy behaviours and to cater for individual differences.

A rich learning environment provides opportunities for children to express their ideas in a variety of ways. Successful classrooms will share most of the following characteristics:

- The furniture is arranged to facilitate different organisational situations, and storage is clearly labelled.
- There is a well maintained and equipped book area with a supply of good-quality fiction and poetry (and possibly non-fiction if this is not stored centrally in the school library).
- A plentiful supply of wide-ranging, interesting books that provide structure and progression in sufficiently small steps to support all reading abilities. The arrangement of the books needs to

be logical (i.e. stored by level of difficulty), clear and accessible. Multiple copies of key books are essential for group reading, and 'big books' are crucial at nursery and reception levels.

- There is an attractive, inviting book corner with a variety of easy-to-read, good-quality, new children's books.
- There is a writing area where children can express thoughts, feelings and ideas.
- All labels and notices are at the appropriate height for the children and are of a high standard for children to emulate.
- A variety of class-made books is easily accessible.
- Audio/visual equipment the children use are easily accessible, e.g. language masters, audio-cassette recorders, 'true image' projectors, etc.
- Computers have concept keyboards and software appropriate for literacy development.
- Reading support materials (including a variety of puzzles and games that encourage word play and a specific focus on print) are ordered and accessible.
- A range of dictionaries, thesauruses and directories is available.
- Wall displays and charts that promote reading and discussion are placed where children can see them.
- There is a listening area with stories on tape, a puppet theatre and storyboards for mini-dramatisations (this is especially important for pupils for whom English is not their first language).
- There are word banks of topic and high-frequency words.
- The class has an enthusiastic and knowledgeable literacy teacher.

Organisation of the children

The teacher of children who are in the early stages of literacy acquisition needs to adopt several ways of working. Working with individual pupils, diagnosing their print-processing competence and monitoring their progress is only one, very important, method. Some activities lend themselves to whole-group teaching. Reading stories (especially with 'big books'), group reading of instructions and the class poem, sharing work at the end of a session, and sound and alphabet work can all be effectively managed in a whole-class or large-group setting.

Teachers need to be flexible in their grouping strategies. Similar-ability groups benefit from working together in group readings, focused phonic work and various writing tasks. Progress needs to be monitored carefully to ensure frequent regroupings, as children make erratic progress spurts in the first years of schooling.

Own-choice groups involving classroom assistants and parents are also useful for such work as book making, language experience activities and games. These groups can take advantage of participants with different reading levels. Needs groups or clusters are for children who have a particular learning need. From time to time these groups should be gathered together for specific skills teaching, such as word recognition practice or phonological development support.

Approaches to literacy teaching within a balanced programme

The half-termly, weekly and daily programme will be planned for literacy activities that capitalise on the ongoing class work or project. Some literacy activities will also be planned that are free standing. A number of primary schools now spend an hour a day on a literacy focus in a concerted effort to devote time and additional adult attention to regular, directed, systematic and rigorous teaching. Integrated literacy activities will, of course, take place at other times and in other aspects of work across the curriculum.

For most of the time, the most valuable learning will take place within a meaningful context and with continuous text. However, the skilled literacy teacher will use a few minutes each day to reinforce systematically phonological and orthographic awareness. Ideally, this should be linked to other work, e.g. a transport project will capitalise on rhyming work with topic words learned by sight: c-*ar*/j-*ar*/p-*ar*/c-*ar*/p-*et*/.

Children may be grouped in differing ways (i.e. whole class, reading level or mixed) for the following suggested activities. One-to-one story sharing can be used for a diagnostic session (see Chapter 3); merely 'hearing children read' is probably an unaffordable luxury with today's pressures on a teacher's time.

A daily programme

To ensure *continous* literacy progress, time needs to be allocated systematically to reading and writing activities. The teacher needs to provide opportunities for the children to

- hear stories;
- read with others;
- read individually either to the teacher or to another adult; and
- practise skills to develop phonological and orthographic awareness.

Each day the teacher needs to make sure he or she

- works with small groups or with individuals;
- considers and provides for the full range of ability in the class;
- finds time to work with children who learn slowly;
- provides for the children who learn more rapidly; and
- monitors the progress of *at least* one child.

Different activities

Reading to children

(This activity can be undertaken with whole-class or smaller same-reading level or mixed-level groups.) Reading to children from stimulating, high-quality and exciting story and non-fiction books is fundamental to any literacy programme. Teachers should use these opportunities to share the enjoyment of a story and the fascination of new ideas to demonstrate that

- reading is an important, culturally required tool;
- delight can be gained from the distinctive nature of book language;
- well written children's literature promotes awareness of ideas and situations not encountered previously, and also develops emotional and moral awareness; and
- reading develops English as an additional language.

Reading books and stories to young children will also reinforce their understanding of the conventions of print ('big books' and 'true image' projectors were discussed in Chapter 2).

Shared reading

(This can be undertaken with whole-class or smaller groups). Shared reading employs the children in a more active role whilst enjoying class stories, 'big books', multiple copies or poems. Developed by Holdaway in the 1960s, the technique emulates the intuitive, preschool book sharing of adult and child, where the child is 'scaffolded' into positive reading behaviours by the adult.

It is well documented that this experience is a powerful learning technique (Ninio and Bruner, 1978). The child is learning (whether in a one-to-one situation, in a small-group or whole-group setting) not only the content of the story or book but also the following are reinforced:

- Understanding of conventions about print.
- Familiarisation with the conventions of punctuation.
- 'Interrogation' of illustrations and text.
- Prediction skills.
- One-to-one spoken word to written word matching.
- Attention to visual details of letters and groups of letters.
- A sight vocabulary of common words.
- A familiarisation with rhythmic and repetitive language.

This activity should occur frequently, four or five times a week, in nursery, reception and Year One classes in addition to daily story reading. The technique is also known as 'read-along','co-operative', 'assisted', 'unison', 'choral' and 'shared' reading. Although they have slight variations, all these have the same learning goal: to support the reading task for the novice reader so that the child can enjoy material he or she is not yet able to tackle alone. In addition, it develops the important strategies of sampling, predicting, confirming and self-correcting for use on text when reading independently. A good story is crucial to withstand repeated collaborative readings.

Introduction to a new shared story

(This can be used with a group of same-level readers.) Book introductions are a valuable way of helping children to predict both context and vocabulary before they attempt to read independently. The teacher can achieve this by 'tuning' the children in to the title, the characters, the illustrations and the possible story line *without* revealing the entire plot. It takes practice and flair to be both enticing towards and informative about a book!

Having introduced a book, the teacher will read the story through, inviting responses and comments on the illustrations. This first reading enables confusions to be straightened out, misunderstandings to be reconciled and prediction skills to be reinforced. The children's knowledge of the world and language (syntax) is drawn upon to

predict words and coming events. As children become more con-
fident and competent, an understanding of grapheme-phoneme associations and the shape and length of words can be encouraged to
confirm or self-correct predictions.

The dissection of the reading process should never be allowed to
diminish the pleasure of the story. The skilled early-years teacher
knows what it is that a given group of children need to know and
need to have emphasised in order to read independently. The teacher
is able to teach and reinforce the precise and appropriate piece of
knowledge *and* enliven the story by reading at exactly the right pace.

Further sharings of the same book

(This can be used with a small group of same-level readers.) Taking
care not to extinguish interest in the story, subsequent book sharing
might lead to further teaching activities:

- Joining in if there is an often-repeated refrain, e.g. 'Oh! No! said
  Mum!', 'We are going on a bear hunt . . .' and 'We can't go over it
  . . .'
- Reading in unison from a strip of card placed at an appropriate
  point in the story the written refrain.
- Reading in unison a commercially produced 'big book'.
- After sharing an enlarged text, individuals can group read with
  small multiple copies at a later date.
- Reading in unison with the audio-taped version.
- After several hearings of the taped version, the text may be at-
  tempted independently.

All these activities rely on the story's strength to sustain interest and
hence to practise and reinforce the development of reading strategies
to gain access to meaning.

Phonological and orthographic awareness work

(The theory and suggestions for skills development in this area of
literacy development will be found in Chapter 2.) Although crucial,
work on this aspect of literacy should not occupy swathes of the
children's time: it is *only* valuable when placed within a balanced
programme. The purpose of this work is to facilitate the *phonemic
segmentation* of words. It also lets children learn how to map the
phonemes on to the graphemes with increasing refinement and

accuracy. Whilst this awareness develops with experience of reading and writing, explicit teaching is also required.

General rhyme and poetry work will help children acquire an appreciation of language, rhyme and rhythms. (For further information, see *Rhyme, Reading and Writing*, edited by Beard (1996), which gives a range of interesting perspectives and practical suggestions.) Goswami and Bryant (1990) have suggested a stage model of the relationship between the development of phonological skills and learning to read (see Figure 5.1). This model explains the connection between rime analogies and progress in literacy. It demonstrates clearly the way literacy development and phonological awareness are circular. In addition, it also shows that phonological awareness supports, and is supported by, orthographic awareness to enhance the accuracy of grapheme-phoneme correspondence.

1) Preschool rhyming and alliteration

Awareness of linguistic units of onsets and rimes

Early reading development (rime analogies)

2) Reading and spelling experience

Increasing specification of phonemes

3) Reading　　　　　　Spelling

(Increasing convergence of strategies)

Figure 5.1　A causal developmental theory of reading
(From Goswami and Bryant, 1990)

Ideas, suggestions and excellent commercially produced materials for teaching rhyme and analogy are now available from Oxford Reading Tree. These were written and produced by Usha Goswami, and are the result of her insightful research work.

Suggestions for practice

It is standard infant practice to write a poem of the week on a large card. This is learned by heart. The children can then recite the poem while the teacher points to the words. Further rhymes can be brain-stormed, e.g. ch-*air*/p-*air*/h-*air*. Through discussion, auditory (or aural) but not orthographic rhyme can be explored, e.g. ch-*air*/p-*ear*.

Phonemic segmentation practice can be done in small, 'same level of reading' groups with whiteboards and felt pens. Words are listened to and then appropriate grapheme choices are made to represent the sound (the choices are made from a limited array of words). Commercially produced charts are available which provide a suggested teaching sequence of grapheme-phoneme correspondence. The following is a *suggested* order for introducing grapheme-phoneme correspondence:

1) *Single letters* and their sounds (identifying both upper and lower case): Aa Bb Cc Dd Ee . . . Xx Yy Zz.
2) *Consonant digraphs* (two consonants that make the same sound/phoneme): *ch, sh, th.*
3) *Consonant blends*: *bl, gl, fl, cl, gr, br*, etc.
4) *Double and triple consonants* (that make the same sound/phoneme): *b-bb, c-k, ck*, etc.
5) *Single vowel* (and its most common sound): a, e, i, o, u.
6) *Vowel digraphs* (two vowels that make the same sound/phoneme): *ai, ay*/*ee, ea, ey*, etc.
7) *Magic e*: a-e/e-e/i-e/o-e/u-e.

Handwriting practice can be used to reinforce the spelling patterns of words being focused on at that time in the class.

The language experience approach

This approach is the time honoured one of all early-years teachers, and it capitalises on children's natural interests and activities and their desire to represent these in spoken language, writing and drawing for themselves and for others. The mechanism is a powerful one:

Experience → Spoken language → Written language → Reading → Rereading

Or

Thought → Spoken language → Encoded into written language → Decoded by reading → Rereading

The power of the 'Language experience approach' derives from the child's interest in the content of the written language generated by him or her and for him or her. In addition, capital can be made of the written language in the natural speech patterns of the child. This approach uses both encoding and decoding processes to effect learning, as each complements and reinforces the other. All the day-to-day class happenings can be captured and used as the talking, reading and writing focus of the day – whether it is the class project, a visit to a place of interest, a visitor contributing to a project, an experiment, biscuits baked, a new baby brother or sister: the permutations are endless. The text can reflect the thoughts of the children or others, the recounting of a happening in the genre of journalism or the retelling of a favourite story using the appropriate narrative language. The resulting product could take the form of a letter, a note, a beautifully crafted handmade book or a large wall story to accompany a picture or model.

The teacher as orchestrator in the 'language experience approach'

The teacher's main role is to be aware of the child and to extend and to support the child consciously both in his or her spoken and written language. The teacher also needs to make explicit the links between spoken and written language in order to effect the bridge that is so powerful for literacy development (Reid, 1993). The quality of the child's language will be determined by the stimulus of the experience and the way in which it is discussed and developed into valuable learning activities. This sensitive way of working with children mimics the adult at home by asking open questions, encouraging the child to reflect and comment further, to hypothesise and, most importantly, to share enjoyment and wonder. As Clay (1979, pp. 53–4) says:

> When we try to provide experiences . . . we must go beyond the usual bounds of spontaneous learning in a free play situation or group learning from one teacher. The child's spontaneous wish to communicate about something which interests him at one particular moment should have priority and he must have adults who will talk with him, in simple, varied and grammatical language. We should arrange for language producing activities where adult and child must communicate to co-operate.

In conclusion

The report by Ofsted (1996, p. 7) on *The Teaching of Reading in 45 Inner London Primary Schools* gives unequivocal advice to schools whose pupils were deemed to be underachieving in terms of progress and attainment as measured by the standardised reading tests used in the inquiry:

> While some things which need to be done to improve matters may require help from outside, there is a great deal that those schools with weak teaching can and should do for themselves. They must above all else focus on the quality of teaching reading in the classroom. Their teachers must be crystal clear as to what their pupils need to know, understand and be able to do to become confident and proficient readers.

This book aims to enable primary teachers to do that.

Bibliography and References

Adams, M.J. (1990) *Beginning to Read: Thinking and Learning about Print.* Cambridge, Mass.: MIT Press.

Adams, M.J. (1991) Why not phonics and whole language? Paper prepared for the Symposium on Whole Language and Phonics, Orton Dyslexia Society, Minneapolis, Minnesota.

Adams, M.J. (1993) Beginning to read: an overview. In R. Beard (ed.) *Teaching Literacy and Balancing Perspectives,* London: Hodder & Stoughton.

Ahlberg, A. and Ahlberg, J. (1986) *The Jolly Postman.* London: Heinemann.

Anastasi, C. (1968) *Psychological Testing,* 3rd ed., New York: The Macmillan Company.

Arnold, H. (1982) *Listening to Children Reading.* Sevenoaks: Hodder & Stoughton.

Aubrey, C. (1993) An investigation of the mathematical competencies which young children bring to school. *British Educational Research Journal,* Vol. 19, pp. 19–27.

Austin, J.J. and Lafferty, J.C. (eds) (1968) *Ready or Not? The School Readiness Checklist Handbook.* Michigan: Research Concepts Test Maker Inc.

Baker, P. and Raban, B. (1991) Reading before and after the early days of schooling. *Reading,* April, pp. 6–13.

Balance Manifesto (1991) *A Manifesto for Balance in the Teaching of Literacy and Language Skills.* Truro: Paul Hamlyn Trust.

Barratt, G. (1986) *Starting School: An Evaluation of the Experience.* Norwich: AMMA.

Beard, R. (1990) *Developing Reading 3–13* (second edition). Sevenoaks: Hodder & Stoughton.

Beard, R. (ed.) (1993) *Teaching Literacy Balancing Perspectives.* London: Hodder & Stoughton.

Beard, R. (ed.) (1996) *Rhyme, Reading and Writing.* London: Hodder & Stoughton.

Beard, R. and Oakhill, J. (1994) *Reading by Apprenticeship? A Critique of the 'Apprenticeship Approach' to the Teaching of Reading.* Slough: NFER.

Bennett, N. (1996) Class size in primary schools: perceptions of headteachers, chairs of governors, teachers and parents. *British Educational Journal of Research,* Vol. 22, pp. 33–55.

Bennett, N., Desforges, C., Cockburn, C. and Wilkinson, B. (1984) *The Quality of Pupil Learning Experiences*. London and Hillsdale, NJ: Lawrence Earlbaum Associates.

Bennett, N. and Kell, J. (1989) *A Good Start? Four Year Olds in Infant Schools*. Oxford: Blackwell.

Berenstein, S. and J. (1979) *The Spooky Old Tree*. London, Collins.

Bialystok, E. (1991) Letters, sounds and symbols: changes in children's understanding of written language. *Applied Psycholinguistics*, Vol. 12, pp. 75–89.

Bielby, N. (1994) *Making Sense of Reading: The New Phonics and its Practical Implications*. Scholastic Publications.

Biemiller, A. (1970) The development of the use of graphic and contextual information as children learn to read. *Reading Research Quarterly*, Vol. 6, pp. 75–96.

Bissex, G.L. (1980) *Gnys at Wrk*. Cambridge, Mass.: Harvard University Press.

Blatchford, P. (1991) Children writing at 7 years: associations with handwriting on school entry and pre-school factors. *British Journal of Educational Psychology*, Vol. 61, pp. 73–84.

Blatchford, P., Burke, J., Farquhar, C., Plewis, I. and Tizard, B. (1987) Associations between pre-school reading related skills and later reading achievement. *British Educational Research Journal*, Vol. 13, pp. 15–23.

Blatchford, P. and Plewis, I. (1990) Pre-school reading related skills and later reading achievement: further evidence. *British Educational Research Journal*, Vol. 16, pp. 425–8.

Bloom, B.S. (1976) *Human Characteristics and School Learning*. New York: McGraw-Hill.

Boehm, A.E. (1967) *The BOEHM Test for Basic Concepts*. New York: The Psychology Corporation (reprinted 1970).

Bond, G.L. and Dykstra, R. (1967) The co-operative research program in first grade reading instruction. *Reading Research Quarterly*, Vol. 2, pp. 5–142.

Bradley, L. and Bryant, P.E. (1983) Categorising sounds and learning to read: a causal connection. *Nature*, Vol. 310, pp. 419–21.

Brimer, M.A. and Dunn, L. (1963) *English Picture Vocabulary Test*. NFER.

Brimer, M.A. and Dunn, L. (1973) *British Picture Vocabulary Test*. NFER.

Brown, S. and Cleave, S. (1994) *Four Year Olds in School. Quality Matters*. Slough: NFER.

Bryant, P.E. and Bradley, L. (1980) Why children sometimes write words which they do not read. In U. Frith (ed.) *Cognitive Processes in Spelling*, New York: Academic Press.

Bryant, P.E. and Bradley, L. (1985) *Children's Reading Problems*. Oxford: Blackwell.

Bryant, P.E., Bradley, L. and Crossland, J. (1989) Nursery rhymes, phonological skills and reading. *Journal of Child Language*, Vol. 16, no. 90, pp. 407–28.

Cashdan, A. (1992) How to teach literacy. *Education*, September, p. 223.

Chall, J.S. (1967) *Learning to Read: The Great Debate*. New York: McGraw-Hill.

Chazan, M., Laing, A. and Jackson, S. (1971) *Just Before School*. Oxford: Blackwell, for the Schools Council.

Chomsky, C. (1971a) Invented spelling in the open classroom. *Word*, Vol. 27, pp. 499–518.

Chomsky, C. (1971b) Write first, read later. *Childhood Education*, Vol. 41, pp. 296–99.

Clark, M.M. (1976) *Young Fluent Readers*. London: Heinemann Educational Books.

Clay, M.M. (1972) *Reading: The Patterning of Complex Behaviour*. London: Heinemann Educational Books. Second edition 1979.

Clay, M.M. (1985) *The Early Detection of Reading Difficulties: A Diagnostic Survey with Recovery Procedures*, 3rd. edn. Portsmouth, NH: Heinemann.

Clay, M.M. (1987) Implementing reading recovery: systematic adaptations to an education innovation. *New Zealand Journal of Education Studies*, Vol. 22.

Clay, M.M. (1991) *Becoming Literate: The Construction of Inner Control*. London: Heinemann.

Clay, M.M. and Cazden, C.B. (1990) A Vygotskian interpretation of reading recovery. In L.C. Moll (ed.) *Vygotsky and Education*, Cambridge: Cambridge University Press.

Cleave, S. and Brown, S. (1991) *Four Year Olds in School*. Slough: NFER.

Cleave, S. and Brown, S. (1994) *Four Year Olds in School: Quality Matters*. Slough: NFER.

Cleave, S., Jowett, S. and Bate, M. (1982) *And So to School*. Windsor: NFER/Nelson.

Clem, K.S. (1990) Moving beyond conflict and confusion in literacy instruction. *Early Child Development and Care*, Vol. 61, pp. 131–8.

Commission on Reading, National Academy of Education (1985) *Becoming a Nation of Readers*. Washington, DC: National Institute of Education.

Dale, E. and Reichert, D. (1957) *Bibliography of Vocabulary Studies*. Columbus, Ohio State University: Bureau of Educational Research.

Daneman, M. (1991) Individual differences in reading skills. In J. Barr, M. Kamil, P. Mosenthal and D. Pearson (eds) *The Handbook of Reading Research*. Vol. 2, London: Longman.

Department for Education (1993) *First Class. The Standards and Quality of Education in Reception Classes. A Report from the Office of HM Chief Inspector of Schools*. London: HMSO.

Donaldson, M. (1978) *Children's Minds*. Glasgow: Fontana.

Donaldson, M. (1989) *Sense and Sensibility: Some Thoughts on the Teaching of Literacy (Occasional Paper 3)*. Reading: Reading and Language Information Centre, University of Reading. Reprinted in Beard, R. (ed.) (1993) *Teaching Literacy Balancing Perspectives*, London: Hodder & Stoughton.

Donaldson, M. and Reid, J. (1985) Language skills and reading: a developmental perspective. In M.M. Clark (ed.) *New Directions in the Study of Reading*, London and Philadelphia, Penn.: Falmer Press.

Downing, J. (1979) *Reading and Reasoning*. Edinburgh: W.C. Books.

Downing, J., Ayers, D. and Schaffer, B. (1984) *Linguistic Awareness in Reading: Readiness Test*. Slough: NFER/Nelson.

Durkin, D. (1966) *Children Who Read Early: Two Longitudinal Studies*. New York: Teachers College Press.

Ehri, L.C. (1983) Summary of Dorothy C. Ohnmacht's study: the effects of letter knowledge on achievement in reading in the first grade. In L.M. Gentile, M.L. Kamil and J.S. Blanchard (eds) *Reading Research Revisited*, Columbus, OH: Charles E. Morrill.

Ehri, L.C. (1995) Phases of development in learning to read words by sight. *Journal of Research in Reading*, Vol. 18, pp. 116–26.

Elliott, C.D. and Pumfrey, P.D. (1991) SATs: sunk, sinking or salvageable? *Education*, Vol. 28, pp.10–11.

Fanthorpe, U.E. (1992) *Heck-Verse, Half-Past Two*. Calstock Poets.

Ferreiro, E. (1985) The relationship between oral and written language: the children's viewpoints, in M.M. Clark (ed.) *New Dimensions in the Study of Reading*, London and Philadelphia: Falmer Press.

Ferreiro, E. and Teberosky, A. (1982) *Literacy Before Schooling*. London: Heinemann.

Ferri, E., Birchall, D., Gingell, V. and Gipps, C. (1981) *The Combined Nursery Centre Project*. Basingstoke: Macmillan Press.

Finn, V.D. and Achilles, C.M. (1990) Answers and questions about class size: a stateswide experiment. *American Educational Research Journal*, Vol. 27, pp. 557–77.

Fisher, R. (1992) *Early Literacy and the Teacher*. UKRA.

Frith, U. (1980) Unexpected spelling problems. In U. Frith (ed.), *Cognitive Processes in Spelling*, New York: Academic Press.

Frith, U. (1985) Beneath the surface of developmental dyslexia. In K.E. Patterson, M. Coltheart and J. Marshall (eds) *Surface Dyslexia*, London: LEA.

Gentry, J.R. (1981) Learning to spell developmentally. *Reading Teacher*, Vol. 34, pp. 378–81.

Gibson, E.J. and Levin, H. (1975) *The Psychology of Reading*. Cambridge, Mass.: MIT Press.

Goodenough, F. (1924) The intellectual factor in children's drawings. Doctoral dissertation, Stanford University, as cited in Eisner, E. (1972) *Educating Artistic Vision* (p. 85). New York: Macmillan.

Goodman, K.S. (1972) Reading: the key is in children's language. *The Reading Teacher*, March, pp. 505–8.

Goodman, K.S. (1973) Psycholinguistic universals in the reading process. In F. Smith (ed.), *Psycholinguistics and Reading*, New York: Holt, Rhinehart & Winston.

Goodman, K.S. (1976) Reading: a psycholinguistic guessing game. In H. Singer and R.B. Ruddell (eds) *Theoretical Models and Processes of Reading*, Newark, Del.: International Reading Association.

Goodman, K.S. and Goodman, Y.M. (1979) Learning to read is natural. In L.B. Resnick and P.A. Weaver (eds) *Theory and Practice of Early Reading*. Vol. 1, Hillsdale, NJ: Lawrence Erlbaum Associates.

Goodman, Y.M. (1980) The roots of literacy. In M.P. Douglass (ed.) *Reading: A Humanising Experience*. Claremont: Claremont Graduate School.

Goodman, Y.M. (1981) Test Review: concepts-about-print tests. *The Reading Teacher*, Vol. 34, pp. 445–8.

Goodman, Y.M. (1986) Children coming to know literacy. In W.H. Teale and E. Sulzby (eds) *Emergent Literacy: writing and reading*, Norwood, NJ: Ablex.

Gorman, T. and Fernandes, C. (1992) *Reading in Recession*. Slough: NFER.

Goswami, U. (1993) Orthographic analogies and reading development. *Bulletin of the British Psychological Society*, Vol. 6, pp. 312–16.

Goswami, U. (1996) Rhyme in children's early reading. In R. Beard (ed.) *Rhyme, Reading and Writing*. London: Hodder & Stoughton.

Goswami, U. and Bryant, P. (1990) *Phonological Skills and Learning to Read*. Hove: Lawrence Erlbaum Associates.

Hall, N. (1987) *The Emergence of Literacy*. Sevenoaks: Hodder & Stoughton.

Harris, D.B. (1969) *Children's Drawings as Measures of Intellectual Maturity, Aneurism and Extension of the Goodenough Draw-a-Man Test*. New York: Harcourt Brace and World.

Hartley, D. and Quine, P. (1982) A critical appraisal of Marie Clay's 'Concepts-About-Print' Test. *Reading*, Vol. 16, no. 2, pp. 109–12.

Hayes, S. (1989) *This is the Bear*. Oxford Reading Tree, Oxford: Oxford University Press.

Heath, S.B. (1982) What no bedtime story means: narrative skills at home and school. *Language in Society*, Vol. 11, pp. 49–76.

HMI (1978) *Primary Education in England: A Survey by HM Inspectors of Schools*. London: HMSO.

HMI (1991) *The Teaching and Learning of Reading in Primary Schools*. London: Department of Education and Science.

Holdaway, D. (1979) *Foundations of Literacy*. Gosford, NSW: Scholastic Publications.

House of Commons Education, Science and Arts Committee (1991) *Standards of Reading in Primary Schools. Third Report of 1990/91 Session. Vol. 1*, London: HMSO.

Hughes, M. (1986) *Children and Number: Difficulties in Learning Mathematics*. Oxford: Blackwell.

Hughes, M., Pinkerton, G. and Plewis, I. (1979) Children's difficulties on starting infant school. *Journal of Child Psychology and Psychiatry*, Vol. 20, pp. 185–96.

Ilg, F.L. and Ames, L.B. (1965) *School Readiness. Behavior Tests used at the Gesell Institute*. New York: Harper & Row.

Inner London Education Authority (1986) *The Junior School Project Part A: Pupils' Progress and Development*. London: ILEA.

Inner London Education Authority (1988) *The Hackney Literacy Study*. London: ILEA.

Johannsen, B.A. (1965) *Criteria of School Readiness (Studies in Educational Psychology)*. Stockholm: Almquist & Wiksell.

Juel, C. (1991) Beginning reading. In J. Barr, M. Kamil, P. Mosenthal and D. Pearson (eds) *The Handbook of Reading Research. Vol. 2*, London: Longman.

Just, M.A. and Carpenter, P.A. (1987) *The Psychology of Reading and Language Comprehension*. Boston, Mass.: Allyn & Bacon.

Mackay, D., Thomson, B. and Shaub, P. (1970) *Breakthrough to Literacy*. Glendale, CA: Bowmar.

Marsh, G., Friedman, M., Welch, V. and Desberg, P. (1980) The development of strategies in spelling. In U. Frith (ed.) *Cognitive Processes in Spelling*, New York: Academic Press.

McGee, L., Lomax, R. and Head, M. (1984) Young children's functional reading. Paper presented at the National Reading Conference, Florida.

McGee, L., Lomax, R. and Head, M. (1988) Young children's written language knowledge: what environmental and functional print reading reveals. *Journal of Reading Behaviour*, Vol. 20, pp. 99–118.

Meek, M. (1982) *Learning to Read*. London: The Bodley Head.

Meek, M. (1988) *How Texts Teach What Readers Learn*. Stroud: Thimble Press.

Merritt, J.E. (1985) The intermediate skills revisited. In M.M. Clark (ed.) *New Directions in the Study of Reading*, Lewes: Falmer Press.

Moll, L.C. (ed.) (1990) *Vygotsky and Education*. Cambridge: Cambridge University Press.

Mortimore, P., Sammons, P., Stoll, L., Lewis, D.R. and Ecob, R. (1988) *School Matters*. London: Paul Chapman.

National Commission for Education (1995) *Learning to Succeed: The Way Ahead*. London: NCE.

Neale, M.D. (1966) *Analysis of Reading Ability*. New York: St Martin's Press.

Neale, M.D. (1989) *The Neale Analysis of Reading Ability* (revised UK edition). Windsor: NFER/Nelson.

Newson, E. and Newson, E. (1977) *Perspectives on School at Seven Years Old*. London: Allen & Unwin.

Ninio, A. (1980) Picture-book reading in mother-infant dyads belonging to two subgroups in Israel. *Child Development*, Vol. 51, pp. 587–90.

Ninio, A. and Bruner, J. (1978) The achievement and antecedents of labelling. *Journal of Child Language*, Vol. 5, pp. 1–15.

Oakhill, J. (1993) Developing skilled reading. In R. Beard (ed.) *Teaching Literacy Balancing Perspectives*, London: Hodder & Stoughton.

Ofsted (1993) *First Class:The Standards and Quality of Education in Reception Classes*. London: HMSO.

Ofsted (1996) *The Teaching of Reading in 45 Inner London Primary Schools*. London: HMSO.

Oppenheim, A.N. (1992) *Questionnaire Design, Interviewing and Attitude Measurement*. London and New York: Pinter Publishers.

Oxford Reading Tree, Oxford: Oxford University Press.

Pedersen, E., Faucher, T.A. and Eaton, W.W. (1978) A new perspective on the effects of first-grade teachers on children's subsequent adult status. *Harvard Educational Review*, Vol. 48, pp. 1–31.

Perfetti, C.A. (1976) Language comprehension and the de-verbalization of intelligence. In L.B. Resnick (ed.) *The Nature of Intelligence*, Hillsdale, NJ.: Lawrence Erlbaum.

Pumfrey, P.D. and Elliott, C.D. (1992) A reaction. *British Psychological Society, Education Section Review*, Vol. 16, pp. 15–19.

Rayner, K. and Pollatsek, A. (1987) Eye movements in reading: a tutorial review. In M. Coltheart (ed.) *Attention and Performance XII: The Psychology of Reading*, London: Lawrence Erlbaum Associates.

Reid, J.F. (1993) Reading and spoken language: the nature of the links. In R. Beard (ed.) *Teaching Literacy Balancing Perspectives*, London: Hodder & Stoughton.

Riley, J.L. (1987) Concepts-about-print Test, adapted from Clay (1972). Unpublished.

Riley, J.L. (ed.) (1992) *The National Curriculum and the Primary School: springboard or straitjacket?* London: Kogan Page.

Riley, J.L. (1994) The development of literacy in the first year of school. Unpublished PhD thesis,University of London.

Riley, J.L. (1995a) The transition phase between emergent literacy and conventional beginning reading: new research findings. *Journal for Tutors for Advanced Courses for Teachers of Young Children.*

Riley, J.L. (1995b) The relationship between adjustment to school and success in reading by the end of the reception year. *Early Child Development and Care*, Vol. 114, pp. 25–38.

Riley, J.L. (1996) The ability to identify and label the letters of the alphabet. *Journal of Research into Reading*, forthcoming.

Sammons, P. (1994) Gender, ethnic and socio-economic difference in attainment and progress: a longitudinal analysis of student achievement over nine years. *British Educational Research Journal*, Vol. 21, pp. 465–85.

Sammons, P., Nuttall, D., Cuttance, P. and Thomas, S. (1995) Continuity of school effects: a longitudinal analysis of primary and secondary school effects on GCSE performance. *School Effectiveness and School Improvement Journal.*

Smith, F. (1971) *Understanding Reading*. New York: Holt, Rinehart & Winston.

Smith, F. (ed.) (1973) *Psycholinguistics and Reading*. New York: Holt, Rinehart & Winston.

Smith, F. (1978) *Understanding Reading* (second edition). New York: Holt, Rinehart & Winston.

Stainthorp, R. (1992) Good theory can also be practically useful: a reply to Turner. *British Psychological Society Education Section Review*, Vol. 16, pp. 19–21.

Stanovich, K.E. (1986) Matthew effects in reading: some consequences of individual differences in the acquisition of literacy. *Reading Research Quarterly*, Vol. 21, pp. 360–406.

Stothard, S. and Hulme, C. (1991) A note of caution concerning the Neale Analysis of Reading Ability (Revised). *British Journal of Educational Psychology*, Vol. 61, pp. 226–9.

Sulzby, E. (1989) Assessment of writing and of children's language while writing. In L. Morrow and J. Smith (eds) *The Role of Assessment in Early Literacy Instruction*, Englewood Cliffs, NJ: Prentice-Hall.

Sulzby, E. (1992) Research directions: transitions from emergent to conventional writing. *Language Arts*, Vol. 69, pp. 291–7.

Sulzby, E. and Teale, W. (1991) Emergent literacy. In J. Barr, M. Kamil, P. Mosenthal and D. Pearson (eds) *The Handbook of Reading Research*, Vol. 2, London: Longman.

Thompson, B. (1975) Adjustment to school. *Educational Research*, Vol. 17, pp. 128–36.

Tizard, B. (1993) Early influences on literacy. In R. Beard (ed.) *Teaching Literacy Balancing Perspectives*, London, Sydney and Auckland: Hodder & Stoughton.

Tizard, B., Blatchford, P., Burke, J., Farquhar, C. and Plewis, I. (1988) *Young Children at School in the Inner City*. Hove and London: Lawrence Erlbaum Associates.

Tizard, B. and Hughes, M. (1984) *Young Children Learning*. London: Fontana.

Turner, M. (1990) *Sponsored Reading Failure*. Warlingham, Surrey: IPSET.

Turner, M. (1991) Finding out. *Support for Learning*, Vol. 6, pp. 99–102.

Turner, M. (1992) Organised inferiority? Reading and the National Curriculum. *British Psychological Society Educational Section Review*, Vol. 16, pp. 1–25.

Vygotsky, L.S. (1962) *Thought and Language*. Cambridge, Mass.: MIT Press.

Vygotsky, L.S. (1978) *Mind in Society: The Development of Higher Psychological Processes*. Cambridge, Mass.: Harvard University Press.

Waterland, L. (1985) *Read with Me: An Apprenticeship Approach to Reading*. Stroud: Thimble Press.

Wells, C.G. (1980) Talking with children: the complementary roles of parents and teachers. In S. Reedy and M. Woodhead (eds) *Family, Work and Education*, Sevenoaks: Hodder & Stoughton Educational with the Open University Press.

Wells, C.G. (1981) *Learning through Interaction*. Cambridge: Cambridge University Press.

Wells, C.G. (1985a) *Language, Learning and Education: Selected Papers from the Bristol Study 'Language at Home and at School'*. Windsor: NFER/Nelson.

Wells, C.G. (1985b) Pre-school literacy related activities and success in school. In G. Oleon, N. Torrance and A. Hildyard (eds) *Literacy, Language and Learning: The Nature and Consequences of Reading and Writing*, Cambridge: Cambridge University Press.

Wells, C.G. (1988) The roots of literacy. *Psychology Today*, Vol. 22, pp. 20–2.

Wells, C.G. and Raban, B. (1978) Children learning to read. Unpublished final SSRC report (lodged in the School of Education Library, University of Bristol).

Willes, M. (1983) *Children into Pupils*. London: Routledge.

Word, E., Achilles, C.M., Bain, H., Folger, J., Johnston, J. and Lintz, N. (1990) Project Star Final Executive Summary: kindergarten through third grade results. *Contemporary Education*, Vol. 62, pp. 13–16.

Appendixes

I   Table of Pearson correlations over time for reading and writing (Tizard *et al.*, 1993, p. 77)

	Nursery (age 4) and age 5 ($n = 247$)	Age 5 and 6 ($n = 346$)	Age 6 and 7 ($n = 288$)	Age 7 and 8 ($n = 256$)	Nursery (age 4) and age 7 ($n = 205$)
Reading	0.57	0.78	0.85	0.89	0.56
Writing	0.50	NA	NA	NA	0.49

II Measures used in the September and July of each academic year

Assessments conducted on the 191 children in the study

The test	Pretest		Administered Post-test	
The BOEHM Test for Basic Concept (1971) Booklet 1 Booklet 2	Sept. '87	Sept. '88	July '88	July '89
The British Picture Vocabulary Test (Brimer and Dunn, 1973)	Sept. '87	Sept. '88	July '88	July '89
The Draw-a-Man Test (Goodenough, revised by Harris, 1963)	Sept. '87	Sept. '88	—	
Concept-About-Print Test (adapted from Marie Clay by author, 1987)	Sept. '87	Sept. '88	July '88	July '89
Knowledge of the Alphabet Test	Sept. '87	Sept. '88	July '88	July '89
Ability to write own (first and family) name or ability to copy first name	Sept. '87	Sept. '88	—	
Neale's Analysis of Reading (1975)	Sept. '87	Sept. '88	July '88	July '89
Thompson *Settled into School* questionnaire completed by teachers (1975)	Nov. '87	Nov. '88	—	

The BOEHM Test for Basic Concepts (Boehm, 1971)
The test was designed to measure children's mastery of basic concepts that are considered necessary for achievement in the first years of school. It purports to test the child's body of knowledge through his or her understandings of concepts such as 'below', 'different', 'middle', 'more', 'top' and 'last'. These terms were selected to assess relatively abstract ideas that would be needed in the curricula areas of reading, maths and science. It tests these understandings and concepts through comprehension of verbal questioning related to a picture booklet. As such, the assessment is of verbal ability as well as conceptual maturity, as it is conducted orally.

The child is not required to make a verbal response but to point to one of the pictures that corresponds to the sentence the examiner gives. Minor anglicising alterations were made to the wording in order to make it more familiar to the child, e.g. 'truck' was changed to 'lorry'. Although the test was designed primarily as a group test for use with 5-year-olds, in the project the researchers administered the test individually, in keeping with the other assessments.

The test takes approximately 15 minutes to administer. The raw scores were used in the analyses.

The short version of the British Picture Vocabulary Test (Brimer and Dunn, 1973)

The BPVS was designed to measure a subject's receptive vocabulary for standard English. The authors claim that it is an achievement test since it shows the extent of English vocabulary acquisition. It provides an estimate of one major aspect of verbal ability for subjects who have grown up in a standard English-speaking environment.

It was chosen as it offers an indication of verbal comprehension and can be regarded as being important to early reading. The BPVS has been standardised on young children in the UK and has been widely used, e.g. the Combined Nursery Centre Project (Ferri *et al.*, 1981). The test also correlated $r = .8$ with an intelligence measure, such as the Stanford Binet (for a normal sample, quoted by Brimer and Dunn, 1973), and so can also be considered an indication of intellectual functioning as vocabulary has been found to be the best single index of school success (Dale and Reichart, 1957).

As a measure of verbal ability, the BPVS is an adaptation of the American Peabody Picture Vocabulary Test and uses American pictures. The authors claim that those pictures that might be unfamiliar to English children were removed from the test (Brimer and Dunn, 1963). Receptive vocabulary is tested by the child being shown a page of four pictures. The child's task is to point to the one that corresponds to the word spoken by the examiner. The short version has been standardised (see Appendix II for details of reliability measures).

The British Picture Vocabulary Scale and the BOEHM Test of Basic Concepts complement each other to give a full picture of the child's baseline of cognitive functioning at school entry. Progress over the year could then be investigated thoroughly rather than a 'snapshot' of attainment at the end of the first year of school.

The Draw-a-Man Test

The original Goodenough Draw-a-Man Test (1924) purported to be a reliable non-verbal measure of intellectual capacity. Goodenough considered that young children's drawings were an indication of conceptual maturity rather than aesthetic content. Harris (1969) revised the test and used a 73-point scale to establish broad age norms. Anastasi (1968) found a high correlation between the test and other measures of reasoning, spatial aptitude and perceptual accuracy.

In this study it was decided to use the test as an indicator of an aspect of intellectual maturity and also as a valuable 'settling down' activity to begin the assessments. A third reason was to invite a child to draw a picture of him or herself, and a logical next step was to label it with his or her own name. This gave a valuable insight into understandings of the distinctness between writing and drawing.

Concepts-About-Print Test

A crucial aspect of learning to read is 'understanding what readers do' (Hall, 1987) and how print functions. The work of Clay (1972) and Downing (1979) gives insight into children's misconceptions about the task of reading. Through exposure to print from their first few months, children gradually develop these concepts about print.

Marie Clay's assessment technique 'Sand' (Clay, 1972) and 'Stones' (Clay, 1979) examines these aspects of reading and knowledge of the conventions of print. The test consists of a 21-page booklet which looks like a story book. It follows the reading book/primer style of text with an illustration on the facing page. As the story progresses odd things begin to happen: illustrations invert, text inverts, lines, words and letters are mixed up. These deliberate 'errors' have clearly caused confusion as publishers find it necessary to inform people that the errors are intentional! This indicates that the assessment technique is contrived and problematic to administer.

Goodman (1981) and Hartley and Quine (1982) reviewed the test and criticised it for being 'unnatural'. Children whom they used it with thought it to be a 'silly' book and frequently refused to respond to what they found to be confusing observations. Goodman suggests that teachers need to adapt the principles behind the test and use them on any good picture book. Riley (1987) devised a test using a 'pop-up' picture book previously unknown to the children, as it was purchased from a publisher's off-set point. The test aims to examine and measure the level of emergent literacy in the following areas:

1) Concepts about book orientation.
2) Concepts about whether print or pictures carry the text message.
3) Concepts about directionality of lines of print, page sequences and directionality of words.
4) Concepts about the relationship between written and oral language.
5) Concepts of words and letters.

This assessment procedure was enjoyed by the children – repetition often demanded and frequently remembered with pleasure from September to July.

Knowledge of the letters of the alphabet (both names and sounds)
Recognising the letters of the alphabet by labelling them with either the names or sounds indicates experience with print, cognitive and perceptual maturity and a developed attention span. This measure was also used to explore the relative value between being able to focus on a specific task of recognition of the alphabet and wider print awareness following the TCRU findings (Tizard *et al.*, 1988).

The measure of letter identification used was similar to that employed by Blatchford *et al.* (1987). The children were shown the 26 letters of the alphabet in both upper and lower case printing (not in alphabetical order). The tester asked, 'Do you know what this letter is?', and on a response of the name, the tester asked, 'Do you know what sound it makes?' If the child supplied the sound the tester asked, 'Do you also know what the name of this letter is?'

The child scored a point for knowing either the name or the sound or two points for knowing both. In the second year of data collection a discrimination was made between letters and sounds in the analyses.

Ability to write or copy own name
The longitudinal *Infant School Study* (Tizard *et al.*, 1988) reported a *r* = .61 correlation between handwriting skills on school entry and reading measured at 7 on the Young Reading Test. The measure of writing ability differed from that used in the TCRU study. The child, after drawing a picture of him or herself, if able, was asked to label it by writing both first and family name. If the child was not able to write even his or her own first name it was written by the tester and the child was invited to copy it. If the child was able to write both names, a maximum of a score of 20 was achieved

given the accuracy, letter formation and spacing. If only the first name was written this was given a maximum of 10 points. If the child copied only, this received a maximum score of 5 points.

The assessment was of a limited aspect of writing ability. However, Blatchford and Plewis (1990) found the preschool handwriting test correlated $r = .5$ ($p < 0.0001$, $n = 206$) with 7-year-old writing test scores in addition to the strong relationship with reading mentioned earlier. The process of writing is the mirror image of the process of reading, and the understandings of literacy develop jointly through exposure to the two activities (Durkin, 1966; Chomsky, 1971a; 1971b).

The standardised reading test

In a study that is investigating progress in reading a measure with a numerical outcome must be used. The choice of test was particularly crucial in this study as the score obtained was to be the dependent variable in the analyses. The author acknowledges the limitations of the use of standardised tests, particularly in the early stages of beginning reading. Criticisms of standardised tests concern the arbitrary nature of a scoring system that one error too many records the child with no reading quotient at all. The choice of vocabulary is crucial in the early stages of reading: chance will dictate whether the result of that individual had a discrepancy between a reading age of 6 or 7 years. Other criticisms of standardised tests from the emergent literacy view of reading would be the artificiality of the testing itself for a very young child, the unknown quality of the text and the unfamiliarity of the researcher. All these factors militate against success or maximum performance, critics claim.

Neale's Analysis of Reading

The Neale's Analysis of Reading is one of the most widely used tests of prose reading ability in the UK. It is used by teachers and psychologists to monitor reading progress (Stothard and Hulme, 1991). It has also been widely used for research purposes (e.g. Bryant and Bradley, 1985).

Reasons for the choice:

1) It is an individually administered test.
2) It looks more like a reading book, with text and supporting illustrations, than a test.
3) It is testing words within a supporting context in contrast to a list of vocabulary (e.g. Schonell).

4) It has a wide reading ability range within its limits (6–13 years reading ages).
5) The format of administration is simple and quick.

The child reads aloud from one to three parallel test sections of progressive reading difficulty. He or she progresses from the earliest level to the one in which more than 16 errors are made. The scoring is achieved by deducting one of the 16 marks awarded to each page, for each error. The child scores a total of 16 marks for each completely correct (error-free) page. The same for each page is totalled and this calculates the raw score. A reading age score is standardised from a conversion table against chronological age. The raw score was used as age was taken into consideration in the analyses for the whole sample of 191. The child scores the lowest score of one, i.e. a reading age of 6.2, if he or she has read the first page with no more than 15 errors.

The standardisation of Neale's Analysis of Reading is its greatest weakness. The test was standardised and first printed in 1958, and the vocabulary and illustrations are rather dated.

Since collecting the data for this study it has been revised (Neale, 1989). The story content has been updated and the presentation style modernised whilst retaining the general format of the original test. However, a note of caution is sounded by Stottard and Hulme (1991). They have misgivings about the reliability of the parallel forms, which they found to yield measures that were not equivalent across the test. They also found Form 2 to be biased against boys. Due to the lack of individual tests available at the time for individual administration for the early stages of reading, it was decided to use the Neale's Analysis of Reading Test. It can be argued that as children are only to be compared with each other within the sample, the issue of standardisation is less important than the necessity of having a reading score in the study.

Assessment of the child's ability to cope with school
It has been shown in Chapter 1 that the child's ability to cope with the discontinuities of the new school situation will inevitably affect learning. 'Readiness is necessary for success' (Austin and Lafferty, 1968), indicating that 'readiness' as a manifestation of social and emotional maturity can be used as a measure of coping ability.

The Thompson *Settled into School* questionnaire (Appendix V) was used as a measure of this ability. The classteacher completed the questionnaire six weeks after the child had been in school.

III   Statistical analyses

The strong relationship between the number of letters the child could identify and label at school entry and reading at the end of the first year of school was demonstrated when the analyses were conducted with each variable (each assessment measure) individually (see Appendix I for the Pearson correlations). Further statistical analyses, step-wise and forced multiple regressions, were also conducted in which the variables were considered together so that both their unique *and* accumulative effect could be measured simultaneously (the relevant multiple regression analyses are in Appendix III).

A summary of Pearson correlation co-efficients between literacy-related entry skills and reading at the end of the year

Identification of letters of the alphabet	*Ability to write own name*	*Concepts about print*
$r = 0.60^*$	$r = 0.57^*$	$r = 0.33^*$

Neale's Analysis of Reading score in July (at the end of the year).

$^*p < 0.001$.

Multiple regression: method step-wise
(Dependent variable = NR2 Neale reading (July post-test))
($n = 191$)

	Variable	*R. square*	*F. change*	
Step 1	Alphabet knowledge	.39	122.41	$p < 0.001$
Beta value .6269				

Adjusted R. square .389

	Variable	*R. square*	*F. change*	
Step 2	Ability to write own name	.05	17.75	$p < 0.001$
Beta value .2578				

Adjusted R. square .44

IV   Chi-square analyses

Chi-square to determine the significance level of the group differences
(n = 191)

	Non-readers	Readers	
Very settled 1	16 (8.4%)	48 (25.1%)	64 (33.5%)
Settling 2	45 (23.6%)	47 (24.6%)	92 (48.2%)
Unsettled 3	28 (14.7%)	7 (3.7%)	35 (16.3%)
	89 (46.6%)	102 (53.4%)	n = 191 (100.0)

Chi-square: 27.88785.
DF: 2.
Significance: $p < 0.001$.
Cells with EF: None.

The figures indicate that there is a statistically significant difference between both those groups of children settled and settling into school and those not so well adjusted and their relative lack of success in reading by the end of the year.

V   *Settled into School* (Thomson) questionnaire

University of London Institute of Education   <u>Confidential</u>

<u>School Reception Class Questionnaire</u>

We are interested in finding out how many of the children entering the
reception class this term are having difficulties of one kind or another
at school and would like your opinion as their class teacher. Would you
please rate this child on each of the following topics <u>by ringing the number</u>
<u>against the statement which you think most applicable</u>. Try to rate each
section independently.

Child's name .... Sex ...... Date of Birth ....

---

1.   <u>Settling in at school</u>

Has settled very well, seems happy in school 4

Has settled quite well, but occasionally shows signs of stress 3

Is gradually settling in but unhappiness and anxiety are still fairly . 2
frequent

Is not settling at all well, is unhappy and unwilling to stay in school 1

---

2.   <u>Cooperation with other children</u>

Very cooperative (usually quite willing and able to cooperate well
e.g. taking on roles in dramatic play, taking share of responsiblity
in group activity) 4

Fairly cooperative (achieves simpler form of cooperation only,
e.g., sharing materials, taking turns, taking part in
simple class games, etc.) 3

Can be cooperative if pleases, but frequently finds difficulty in sharing
materials, taking turns 2

Uncooperative (cannot or will not share materials, take turns in play,
class games, etc.. May disrupt activity of others or be afraid of
other children) 1

---

3.   <u>The child's relationship with you, the teacher</u>

Has a very friendly and responsive relationship 4

Is friendly and responsive on the whole 3

Is occasionally responsive but never initiates contact 2

Uncertain in contacts - shy, withdrawn or hostile 1

---

4. Level of concentration

Concentrates very well for quite long periods; ignores distractions .. 4

Usually concentrates quite well, but sometimes loses interest and
attention wanders 3

Seldom able to concentrate for long but occasionally something
catches interest 2

Usually lacks concentration, e.g., concentrates for a few minutes only,
easily distracted 1

5. Use of play materials

Play usually leads to end product (e.g. model or painting) or successful
completion of activity 4

Play sometimes leads to end product/successful completion of activity 3

Play rarely leads to end product or successful completion of activity 2

Almost entirely unable to use play materials constructively 1

6. Self Reliance

Likes to work things out for self; seeks help from the teacher or other
children only as a last resort 4

Will cope unaided with the straightforward or reasonably familiar but soon
looks around for help when a situation is difficult or novel 3

Will attempt very little without guidance or reassurance from the
teacher 2

Seems content to remain helpless and therefore dependent on the
teacher 1

7. Verbalising ability in school work

Able to describe own thoughts and actions fluently 4

Generally able to describe own thoughts and actions but further questions
often needed to make meaning clear 3

Can form simple sentences only and has poor level of vocabulary to describe
thoughts and actions 2

Is incoherent and rambling or remains silent 1

8. Following instructions

Never has much difficulty in understanding an instruction or request from
the teacher 4

Grasps the meaning of a complex or lengthy instruction only if it is
repeated 3

Sometimes the teacher has to repeat even brief or simple instructions before
he/she understands 2

Several repetitions are usually necessary before he/she understands an
instruction or request 1

9. Ability to cope with personal needs

Can dress self and care for ordinary toilet needs without assistance . 4

Seldom needs assistance with these activities 3

Is beginning to cope with clothing and toilet needs but may frequently ask for assistance 2

Requires constant help if these needs are to be taken care of 1

---

10. Sociability

Very friendly and responsive to other children 4

Friendly and responsive to other children on the whole 3

Somewhat isolated. Rarely initiative contact with other children 2

Very isolated. Has great difficulty relating to other children 1

---

11. Physical Coordination

Very well coordinated and physically agile 4

Well coordinated on the whole 3

Rather uncoordinated. Tends to be clumsy 2

Very poorly coordinated. Very clumsy 1

---

12. Fine motor control

Very controlled use of pencil for drawing or writing 4

Is able to use pencil for drawing or writing with moderate control ... 3

Has some difficulty using a pencil for drawing or writing 2

Has great difficulty using a pencil for drawing or writing and has very little control 1

IN GENERAL would you say that this child is

Coping very well with school 4

Coping adequately with school 3

Having some difficulty coping with school (causing some concern to you) 2

Having major difficulties coping with school (causing a lot of concern to you) 1

Are there any particular comments you would like to make about this child?

VI   Questionnaire sent to reception teachers

QUESTIONNAIRE INTO READING IN THE FIRST YEAR OF SCHOOL

1   Please indicate your declared aims of the reception year of school

(a)   **Mainly academic**

least
important
/_____/_____/_____/_____/_____/
most
important

(b)   **Mainly social**

least
important
/_____/_____/_____/_____/_____/
most
important

2   Does the emphasis change during the year?

A great deal   Yes, somewhat   No, not at all

☐   ☐   ☐

If yes – how does it change?

3   How has the National Curriculum affected your aims of the first
year of school?

4   List below skills or understandings that facilitate learning to read

☐

_____

☐

_____

☐

_____

☐

_____

☐

_____

Now please rank them in order of importance by numbering to the right

5   Within the first month of school what are the criteria you use to assess
         where the child is in reading?

         _____   ☐

         _____   ☐

         _____   ☐

         _____   ☐

         _____   ☐

         Now please rank in order of importance by numbering in the boxes to the right
                    (5 for the most important)

6   What do you hope that parents/carers or nursery schools have taught the child
         about literacy before s/he comes to you?

         _____   ☐

         _____   ☐

         _____   ☐

         _____   ☐

         _____   ☐

         Now please rank in order of importance by numbering in the boxes to the right

7   What different methods or ways into the teaching of early reading do you use?

8   Which of the following entry skills do you consider to be most important in facilitating development of reading? (Please number them in rank order of importance i.e. 4 is most important and 1 is least important.)

RANK

Spoken Language

Concepts about print (understandings of the way books and print works, L-R direction, etc.)

Knowledge of the alphabet

Ability to write name

Any Comments

VII   The mean scores of pupils over the whole sample

**Mean scores of the pre-test (entry skills) and post-test (exit skills)
over the whole sample**
n = 191

Test		Pre-Test (entry skills Sept '87/'88)	Post-test (exit skills July '88/'89)
BOEHM Test	Mean	20.28	22.64
of Basic Concepts	SD	3.96	2.58
Booklet 1	Min.	5	8
	Max.	25	25
	Range	20	17
BOEHM Test	Mean		15.85
of Basic Concepts	SD		4.28
Booklet 2	Min.		4
	Max.		23
	Range		19
B.P.V.S.	Mean	11.78	14.39
British Vocabulary	SD	3.07	7.88
Test	Min.	5	6
	Max.	21	27
	Range	16	21
Concepts-about-	Mean	6.35	10.25
print	SD	2.79	2.40
	Min.	0	3
	Max.	12	12
	Range	12	9
Alphabet	Mean	9.45	14.59
Knowledge	SD	10.45	7.88
	Min.	0	8
	Max.	26	26
	Range	26	18
Ability to write	Mean	12.27	
name	SD	7.00	
	Min.	0	
	Max.	25	
	Range	25	
Draw-a-man test	Mean	59.28	
	SD	10.97	
	Min.	30	
	Max.	96	
	Range	66	
Neale's Analysis	Mean	.754	6.14
of Reading	SD	3.5	8.68
	Min.	0	0
	Max.	31	31
	Range	31	31
Thomson School	Mean	20.64	
Adjustment Score	SD	6.21	
	Min.	13	
	Max.	44	
	Range	31	
Age	Mean	60.15 (months)	
	SD	3.50	
	Min.	49 (months)	
	Max.	68 (months)	
	Range	19	

VIII Scores of the pupils in the four case-study teachers' classes

(n = 9)

Individual pupil's scores from one class indicating progress achieved

Teacher: Vera

School: Rural

Child	Aymer	Thomas	Ian	Glenn	Vanessa	Lewis	Nicholas	Julia	Eleanor	Sept. 1988	July 1989
Boehm (1)	24	16	19	14	17	23	16	23	24	19.5 SD 3.9	
Boehm (2)	25	23	25	21	22	25	20	25	25		23.4 SD 2.0
Boehm (3) (July only)	22	19	22	11	15	16	12	19	21		16.3 SD 4.8
Neale's Analysis of Reading Sept	0	0	0	0	0	0	0	0	0		
July	8.0	7.11	7.2	6.5	6.3	6.6	0	7.6	6.10	0.0	75.4 (6.3) SD 29.3
C.A.P. Sept	9	5	5	5	7	5	4	8	8	6.2 SD 1.7	
July	12	12	12	12	12	10	12	12	12		11.7 SD .6
B.P.V.S. Sept	113	116	121	104	94	83	104	123	91	105.4 SD 13.9	
July	135	124	135	106	109	132	109	114	113		119.7 SD 11.8
Name Sept	25	10	5	3	3	15	10	3	20	11.5 SD 7.0	
Motor Control	Poor	Mod.	Mod.	Poor	Mod.	Mod.	Poor	Mod.	Mod		
Letters - names and sounds Sept	10s 26n	6s 23n	19s 5n	1s 3n	9s16n	0s 14n	0s 0n	2s 1n	0s 7n	n 10.5 s 5.2 SD=9	
July	16s 26n	15s 24n	22s 24n	16s 4n	11s 26n	0s 23n	0s 15n	0s 21n	1s 20n		n 20.33 s 9.0 SD 7.0
D.A.M. Sept	5.5	5.0	5.75	3.5	3.75	5.0	4.0	4.75	5.25	56.4 SD 9.6	
Age Sept	5.0	5.2	5.3	4.11	5.1	4.11	5.1	5.0	4.10	61.4 5.1 SD 6.1	
Gender	M	M	M	M	F	M	M	F	F		

Individual pupil's scores from one class indicating progress achieved

Teacher: Annette

School: Rural

Child	Havley	Vicky	Leanne	Agnes	Neil	Christopher	Sept. 1988	July 1989
Boehm (1)	23	24	23	25	22	4	21.8 SD 3.9	23.2 SD 2.6
Boehm (2)	23	25	24	25	24	18		23.2 SD 2.6
Boehm (3) (July only)	13	19	13	23	21	15		17.3 SD 4.2
Neale's Analysis of Reading Sept	0	0	0	0	0	0	0	
July	6.2	6.5	6.7	7.10	8.9	0		70.3 (5.10) SD 35
C.A.P. Sept	6	6	6	8	9	2	6.1 SD 2.4	11.0 SD 2.4
July	12	12	12	12	12	6		
B.P.V.S. Sept	113	116	111	111	126	88	110.8	114.0
July	106	104	109	114	130	121	SD 12.5	SD 9.0
Name	20	15	15	20	20	5	15.8 SD 5.8	
Motor Control	Good	Good	Good	Good	Mod.	Poor		
Letters - names and sounds Sept	0s 5n	0s 3n	0s 5n	13s 2n	13s 3n	0s 0n	3.00 SD 1.8 4.3 SD 6.7	
July	0s 25n	0s 25n	1s 23n	22s 16n	21s 4n	18n		19.5 SD 8.0 6.3 SD 9.0
Draw-a-man Sept	5.25	5.5	5.5	5.5	4.5	3.75	59.3 (4.11)	
Settled Sept	51	52	46	39	44	41	45.5 SD 5.2	
Age Sept	5.1	5.3	5.3	5.4	5.2	5.1	62.3 (5.2)	
Gender	F	F	F	F	M	M		

(n = 9)

Individual pupil's scores from one class indicating progress achieved

Teacher: Janet

School: Inner City

Child	Rowena	Sara	Louis	Nicola	James	Philipry	Robert	Yoland	Gerard	Sept 1988	July 1989
Boehm (1)	25	17	16	21	16	24	15	17	16	18.5	
Boehm (2)	25	22	25	23	22	25	16	21	24		22.5
Boehm (3) (July only)	19	15	16	13	13	22	15	10	11		14.6
Neale's Analysis of Reading Sept	0	0	0	0	0	0	0	0	0		
July	6.11	0	0	0	0	7.0	0	0	0		(18.5 mths)
C.A.P. Sept	12	6	7	8	5	10	3	5	7	6.3	
July	12	8	8	8	9	12	8	4	7		8.4
B.P.V.S. Sept	106	93	91	102	99	111	101	91	86	97.7 SD 8.1	
July	126	94	111	108	101	123	88	83	103		104.1 SD 4
Name	20	0	5	10	0	20	5	5	10	8.7 SD 7.3	
Motor control	Mod	Poor	Poor	Poor	Poor	Mod.	Poor	Mod.	Poor		
Letters - names & sounds Sept	25s 0n	0s 1n	0s 2n	0s 26n	0s 0n	26s 26n	0s 0n	0s 0n	0s 0n	5.5s 6.4n	
July	25s 26n	0s19n	0s 9n	0s 26n	0s 2n	26s 26n	0s 12n	0s 2n	0s 9n		5.6s 13.7n
Draw-a-man Sept	5.75	4.0	3.75	3.75	4.5	5.0	4.0	5.25	3.5	(4yr 4)	52.2 (4.4)
Settled Sept	40	42	30	47	29	46	40	33	39	38.4	
Age Sept	4.5	4.3	4.10	4.1	4.11	4.9	4.7	4.1	4.8	4.6	5.4
Gender	F	F	M	F	M	M	M	F	M		

(n = 8)

Individual pupil's scores from one class indicating progress achieved

Teacher: Wanda

School: Inner City

Child	Saran	Emily	John	Michelle	Jonathan	Billy	Robin	Jock	Sept 1988	July 1989
Boehm (1)	23	24	22	14	25	18	18	24	21 SD 3.8	
Boehm (2)	24	23	24	21	25	21	23	24		23.2 SD 1.4
Boehm (3) (July only)	19	17	16	10	24	9	14	19		16.00 SD 4.9
Neale's Analysis of Reading Sept	0	0	0	0	7.3	0	0	6.8	20.6 SD 38.2	
July	6.7	6.7	0	0	8.1	0	0	6.9		40.7 SD 44.2
C.A.P. Sept	11	10	12	3	9	7	7	10	9.0 SD 3.1	
July	12	12	12	10	12	9	8	12		10.8 SD 1.6
B.P.V.S. Sept	113	109	99	97	116	94	88	106	102.7 SD 9.7	
July	111	121	106	93	116	106	91	123		108.3 SD 11.8
Name Sept	20	15	15	5	20	10	10	20	14.3 SD 5.6	
Motor Control Sept	Mod.	Mod.	Poor	Poor	Mod.	Poor	Poor	Mod.		
Letters - names and sounds Sept	1s 9n	5s 10n	0s 3n	0s 11n	0s 26n	0s 3n	0s 0n	17s 2n	n 8.0 s 2.8	
July	26s 26n	26s 26n	0s 12n	0s 19n	26s 26n	0s 9n	0s 13n	26s 26n		n 19.6 s 13.0
Draw-a-man	6.5	6.0	6.25	5.0	5.25	5.5	3.5	5.75	64.6 SD 11.4	
Settled Sept	47	52	44	45	42	41	48	50	46.1 SD 3.8	
Age Sept	4.11	5.0	5.0	4.9	4.10	5.0	5.0	4.9	4.10	5.8
Gender	F	F	M	F	M	M	M	M		

IX   Examples of 'running reading records'

RUNNING RECORD SHEET

Name: __James__   Date: _17-10-95_ D. of B.: _____ Age: _6_ yrs _3_ mtr

School: _____   Recorder: _____

Text Titles	Running words / Error	Error rate	Accuracy	Self-correctic rate
1. Easy _____	$\frac{33}{3}$	1: _____	_____ %	1: _____
2.(4) Instructional _Washing_	$\frac{3}{3}$	1: _11_	_9C_ %	1: _4_
3. Hard _____		1: _____	_____ %	1: _____

Directional movement _____

Analysis of Errors and Self-corrections
Information used or neglected [Meaning (M) Structure or Syntax (S) Visual (V)]

Easy _____

Instructional _James attended well to meaning and to the language and story structure. At times he neglected print information_

Hard _____

Cross-checking on information (Note that this behaviour changes over time)

He was able to self-correct once making use of the illustration and checking the initial letter j

Analysis of Errors and Self-correction: (see *Observation Survey* pages 30–3:

Page	Washing						E	SC	E MSV	SC MSV
8	✓	—	✓	trousers / SC jumper /			1		Ⓜ Ⓢ V	Ⓜ S Ⓥ
4	✓	—	—	—						
5	✓	✓	✓	jumper trousers			1		Ⓜ Ⓢ V	
6	✓	✓	—	—						
7	✓	✓	✓	$\frac{red}{—}$	✓		1		Ⓜ Ⓢ V	
8	✓	✓	⌣	$\frac{Teddy}{Ted}$			1		Ⓜ Ⓢ Ⓥ	
9	✓	✓	—	✓						
10	✓	—	✓	✓	✓					

| Page | Washing: Ginn All Aboard Stage 1 | E | SC | Information used | |
				E MSV	SC MSV

In went my jumper.

In went my shirt.

In went my trousers.

In went my skirt.

In went my slippers.

In went my Ted.

They all went round

and they all went red.

RUNNING RECORD SHEET

Name: __Joanna__   Date: __9-11-95__ D. of B.: _____ Age: ____ yrs ____ mtr

School: _____   Recorder: _____

Text Titles	Running words / Error	Error rate	Accuracy	Self-correctic rate
1. Easy _____	_____	1: _____	_____ %	1: _____
2. Instructional _____	_____	1: _____	_____ %	1: _____
3.⑤ Hard __The toys' party__	__48/5__	1: __9__	__89__ %	1: __2__

Directional movement _____

Analysis of Errors and Self-corrections
Information used or neglected [Meaning (M) Structure or Syntax (S) Visual (V)]

Easy _____

Instructional _____

Hard __Joanna was paying close attention to the storyline throughout, and made good use of her strong oral language. She attended to print cues__

Cross-checking on information (Note that this behaviour changes over time) __variably.__

__Additional print information and flexible attention to meaning led Joanna to correct half her errors.__

Analysis of Errors and Self-corrections (see *Observation Survey* pages 30–3̃

Page	The toys' party	E	SC	Information used E MSV	SC MSV
1	✓ ✓ ✓				
2	Every | sc / Nobody | — make / come		1	ⓂⓈv Ⓜ s Ⓥ �/ ⓂⓈv	
4	✓ ✓ ✓ teddies | sc / toys	1		ⓂⓈⓋ	M s Ⓥ
6	✓ / went |R| sc ✓ birthday ✓ / wanted | —	1 1		ⓂⓈⓋ / ⓂⓈ v	M s Ⓥ
8	✓ ✓ ✓ cocopops |A| / cornflakes | |T	1		ⓂⓈⓋ	
9	✓ ✓ ✓ ✓ ketchup / sauce	1		ⓂⓈv	
10	✓ ✓ ✓ ✓				

Analysis of Errors and Self-corrections
(see *Observation Survey* pages 30–32)

Page		E	SC	Information used E MSV	SC MSV
11	✓ ✓ ✓ ✓				
12	✓ ✓ ✓ ✓				
13	✓ ✓ ✓ beans / sc baked		1	(M) (S) (V) M s (V)	
14	✓ saw / sc was angry cross		1 1	(M)(S)(V) (M) s (V) (M)(S) v	
16	✓ ✓ ✓				

The toys' party · Oxford Reading Tree · Stage 2.

1. Kipper wanted a party.
2. Nobody wanted to come.
4. He got his toys.
6. He wanted a cake.
8. He put in cornflakes.
9. He put in tomato sauce.
10. He put in milk.
11. He put in jam.
12. He put in sugar.
13. He put in baked beans.
14. Mum was cross.
16. Kipper was sorry.

RUNNING RECORD SHEET

Name: __Nadia__   Date: __25-1-96__ .D. of B.: _____   Age: _____ yrs _____ mtr

School: _____   Recorder: _____

Text Titles	Running words / Error.	Error rate	Accuracy	Self-correctio. rate
1. Easy _____	_____	1: _____	_____ %	1: _____
2.⑧ Instructional __Mrs. Wishy-Washy__	$\frac{94}{6}$	1: __15__	_____ %	1: __2·5__
3. Hard _____	_____	1: _____	_____ %	1: _____

Directional movement _____

Analysis of Errors and Self-corrections
Information used or neglected [Meaning (M) Structure or Syntax (S) Visual (V)]

Easy _____

Instructional __Nadia was able to use all sources of information, re-running at times to pull the story together. Still neglects print at times.__

Hard _____

Cross-checking on information (Note that this behaviour changes over time)

Used more print cues together with the story line to change her original responses.

Analysis of Errors and Self-corrections (see *Observation Survey* pages 30–3.

Page	Mrs. Wishy-Washy	E	SC	Information used E MSV	SC MSV
2	✓ ✓ ✓ / ✓ ✓ ✓				
3	✓ ✓ ✓ ✓ ✓				
A	✓ R what | sc ✓ lovely |				
	✓ ✓ big | sc pig |	1		Ⓜ Ⓢ v	M S Ⓥ
		1		Ⓜ Ⓢ Ⓥ	M S Ⓥ
5	✓ ✓ ✓ ✓ ✓				
6	✓ look | R | what | sc ✓ lovely |	1		Ⓜ Ⓢ Ⓥ	M S Ⓥ
	✓ ✓ ✓			Ⓜ Ⓢ V	M S Ⓥ

Analysis of Errors and Self-corrections
(see *Observation Survey* pages 30–32)

Page		E	SC	E MSV	SC MSV
				Information used	
7	↙ ✓ R				
	jumped / paddled ✓ —	l		(M) (S) V	
8	✓ ✓				
9	What / Just |T did/look /sc ✓ ✓	l	l	(M) (S) V / (M) S V (M)(S)(V)	
	✓R shouted / screamed	l		(M) (S)(V)	
10	✓ ✓ bath/tub ✓ ✓	l		(M) (S) V	
11	✓R ✓ ✓ — ✓ —				
12	✓ R₂ ✓ ✓ — ✓ ✓				
13	✓ ✓ — — ✓ ✓				
14	Good/That's | The | T good/better	l		(M) (S) U / M S (U)	
	✓ ✓ ✓ ✓ ✓ — ✓ ✓	l		(M) (S) U	
15	✓ ✓ ✓ — ✓ — — — ✓ — ✓ —				
16	✓ ✓ — ✓ ✓				

Mrs. Wishy-Washy : Nelson Storychest

2. "Oh, lovely mud,"
   said the cow,

3. and she jumped in it.

4. "Oh, lovely mud,"
   said the pig,

5. and he rolled in it.

6. "Oh, lovely mud,"
   said the duck,

7. and she
   paddled in it.

8. Along came
   Mrs. Wishy-Washy.

9. "Just look at you,"
   she screamed.

10. "In the tub you go."

11. In went the cow,
    wishy-washy, wishy-washy.

12. In went the pig,
    wishy-washy, wishy-washy.

13. In went the duck,
    wishy-washy, wishy-washy.

14. "That's better,"
    said Mrs. Wishy-Washy,
    and she went into
    the house.

15. Away went the cow.
    Away went the pig.
    Away went the duck.

16. "Oh lovely mud,"
    they said.

RUNNING RECORD SHEET

Name: _Damari_   Date: _14-12-95_ D. of B.: _____ Age: ____ yrs ____ mtr

School: _____   Recorder: _____

Text Titles	Running words / Error	Error rate	Accuracy	Self-correction rate
1. Easy _____	$\frac{112}{6}$	1: _____	_____ %	1: _____
2.⑭ Instructional _Ten garden snails_		1: _18_	_94_ %	1: _1·5_
3. Hard _____	_____	1: _____	_____ %	1: _____

Directional movement _____

Analysis of Errors and Self-corrections
Information used or neglected [Meaning (M) Structure or Syntax (S) Visual (V)]

Easy _____

Instructional _Damari is working flexibly with all information source_
She sometimes neglects to make full use of meaning, but her
reading is driven well by oral languag

Hard _____

Cross-checking on information (Note that this behaviour changes over time)
She can often pull together print information using her understand
of the story and spoken language. She also Analysis of Errors and Self-corrections
makes several attempts using more print info (see *Observation Survey* pages 30–3

Page	Ten little garden snails	E	SC	Information used E MSV	SC MSV
2	✓ ✓ ✓ ✓ ✓ ✓ ✓ garden|green/sc ✓ R grey		1	Ⓜ Ⓢ Ⓥ Ⓜ S Ⓥ	Ⓜ S v
4	ten|sc ci|sc ✓ ✓ ✓ ✓ two climbed ✓ there|sc then		1 1 1	Ⓜ Ⓢ E M S Ⓥ Ⓜ Ⓢ Ⓥ	Ⓜ S Ⓜ Ⓢ M S Ⓥ
6	✓ ✓ ✓ ✓ ✓ ✓ ✓ shell|shelf|sh t/ sticks | | T ✓ ✓ ✓ ✓ ✓ ✓ ✓ ✓		1	M S Ⓥ	

Analysis of Errors and Self-corrections
(see *Observation Survey* pages 30–32)

Page		E	SC	E MSV	SC MSV
				Information used	
8	et / eating | ěting / eating | R | sc ✓ — — —		1	M S (V)	(M)(S) u
	✓ ✓ — sp·ct d / spotted | sc ✓		1	M s (v)	(M)(S) v
10	✓ ✓ — — —			M S (V)	●
	✓ ✓ ✓ went / wet |T dow / dew děw |T	1 1	M s (V) M s (V)	
	— ✓ hen / hungry | sc ✓		1	(M)(S)(V) M s (V)	
	✓ ✓ ✓ ✓				
12	✗ — flōw / flower | fl | R | fly | flor |T ✓		1	M s (V)	
14	✓ ✓ w i t· / white | sc ✓		1	M S (V) (M)(S) v	
	✓ ✓ s,e,c· / secret | sc s·p· / spot | soap |T		1 1.	M S (V) M (S)(V)	(M)(S) v ●
16	✓ ✓ ✓ — —				
	hatching / hidden | h·i·den | sc for / from ✓ ✓		1 1	(M)(S)(V) M s (v) M (S)(V)	(M)(S) v
	✓ — — — ✓				
	✓ ✓ — pl·a·ge / page | sc ✓		1	M s (V)	(M)(S) v

Ten little garden snails : Nelson One-to-One Stories

2. 10 little garden snails
    by the old grey gate . . .

4. two climbed and saw the sun,
    and then there were 8.

6. 8 little garden snails
    hiding in the sticks . . .
    two met a hedgehog,
    and then there were 6.

8. 6 little garden snails
    eating more and more . . .
    two met a spotted bird,
    and then there were 4.

10. 4 little garden snails
     in the cold wet dew . . .
     two met a hungry hen,
     and then there were 2.

12. 2 little garden snails
     on a flower pot . . .   (mating!)

14. went to hide
     some round white eggs
     in a secret spot!

16. 10 little round white eggs
     hidden from the sun . . .
     Now the story starts again!
     Go back to page 1.

Subject Index

miscue analysis, 60–1
monitoring, xiii, 51–2, 54, 56, 59–61, 75, 82, 84
'moving word', 13

name, child's own, xv, 103–4, 114–18
naturalness, 20–1
Neales Analysis of Reading Test, 104, 106, 114–18

observation, 30, 49, 51–3, 57–61, 71–2, 75, 81
onset, 17, 28, 33, 35, 38, 87
orthography, xiv, xvi, 9–15, 17, 23, 26–7, 33, 35, 37–8, 51, 54–5, 57–8, 83–4, 86–7

phased start, 71
phonology, xiv, 17, 23–4, 28, 32–3, 35, 37–8, 51, 58, 83–4, 86–7
play, 80
poem of the week, 87–8
prediction, 19, 21, 32, 34, 36, 38, 40, 53–6, 60, 77–8, 85–6
prereading, 7
preschool, 70
'pretend' reading, 50
punctuation, 85

reading to children, 84
reading models, 19–29
reading schemes, 21, 24, 50, 74, 76
real books, 21
rhyme, 17, 28, 32, 35, 37–8, 49, 83, 87–8
rhythm, 77, 85
rime (*see also* rhyme), 10, 28, 35, 38, 87

running reading records, 60–1, 119–28

sampling, 53–6, 60, 78, 85
scaffolding, 5, 8, 38, 52, 85
scanning, 36, 78
segmentation, phonemic, 10, 14, 28, 32–3, 35, 49–50, 60, 79, 86
self-correction, 36, 38, 54–6, 60, 78, 85–6
sequencing, 50
shared reading, *see* interactive reading
socialisation, 63
socioeconomic background, 43, 46, 65
special educational needs, 41, 46
spoken language, 1, 17, 23–5, 40, 45, 54, 79–80
stage theory, 9
storying, 50, 80
success, school, 6–7
symbolism, 13–14, 47, 50

teachers and staffing, xii–xiv, 48–51, 64, 71–3, 74–5, 83, 90
thought, 6
'top-down' models, 19, 22–3
transition, to school, xi, xiii, 5, 45, 62–73, 105, 107, 108–10, 114–18

vocabulary, 1, 77–8, 80, 101, 104
sight, 34, 36–8, 50, 53–4, 59–60, 85

whole language, 20–2
written text, 79–80

zone of proximal development, 5

Author Index